ENVELOPES

ENVELOPES

ENVELOPES

A Puzzling Journey Through the Royal Mail

HARRIET RUSSELL

Foreword by Lynne Truss

RANDOM HOUSE · NEW YORK

Published in the United States by Random House, an imprint of
The Random House Publishing Group, a division of
Random House, Inc., New York.

RANDOM HOUSE and colophon are registered trademarks
of Random House, Inc.

ROYAL MAIL is the registered trademark of Royal Mail Group plc.
Stamp imagery © Royal Mail Group plc 1998–2004.
Reproduced by kind permission of Royal Mail.
All rights reserved.

Library of Congress Cataloging-in-Publication Data

Russell, Harriet
Envelopes/Harriet Russell.
p.   cm.
ISBN 1-4000-6400-7
1. Letters in art. 2. Conceptual art—Great Britain.
3. Envelopes, Addressing of—Miscellanea. I. Title.
NC242.R85A4 2005
741.6'092—dc22   2005040710

Printed in China on acid-free paper
www.atrandom.com

2 4 6 8 9 7 5 3 1

FIRST EDITION

Book design by Carole Lowenstein

A NOTE FROM THE ROYAL MAIL

This book highlights how the Royal Mail's postmen and women often go beyond the call of duty to deliver poorly addressed mail. Each week they successfully deliver 15 million badly addressed letters, and our Return Letter Centre—where items are opened with the hope of finding a return address—handles a further 72 million undeliverable items a year. To help us deliver your post, can we remind you to clearly and correctly address items being posted. Thank you.

Challenging the Postal system,
(Particularly the Postman
who delivers to Flat 1/1 17
Montague St G4 9HV)
Harriet Russell, 1999

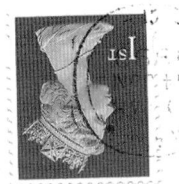

FOREWORD

I can't remember the last time I sent a letter to myself. Generally, the act of auto-mailing is committed only a) if you are entirely friendless, but pathetically want to pretend otherwise; b) in quite complicated legal circumstances, when a sealed, registered self-sent envelope can be used as proof of dating; or c) by mistake, when drunk.

Sending oneself letters in the cause of larky art is quite a new idea, therefore, and Harriet Russell is to be thoroughly congratulated for coming up with it. Having lived for years at the quite challenging address "Shulbrede Priory, Linchmere, Haslemere, Surrey, GU27 3NQ", she noticed that correspondence often successfully reached the house despite any old mis-spelled, inadequate, wild-stab nonsense scrawled on the envelope, and was impressed by what this revealed about the sturdy broad-mindedness of staff at the Royal Mail, not to mention their excellent sense of humour and saintly forbearance. She realised that if you were to write "Shawl Bird Puree, Finch More, Hazy More, Curry, GU27 3NQ" on an envelope, and illustrate each word with a little coloured drawing, it would not only certainly reach the house, but might provide considerable entertainment along the way, as well.

So that's what she did. She embarked on this witty project, "Envelopes", in which each envelope represents a new, delightfully clever idea to hide or disguise the address, and is also a little triumph of humanity—because, after all, in nearly every case, the letter arrived! Therefore, a human person must have worked out Harriet's code, or enjoyed the conceit, or (at the very least) held the envelope at arm's length, recognising the handiwork of that annoying woman in that flat in Montague Street. I like the envelope that shows Harriet's Glasgow address in mirror-writing, with the stamp in the top-left corner, instead of the top-right. "Please postmark here" Harriet has written, back to front, next to the stamp. And the Royal Mail has obliged. Maybe it was the work of a machine. You can't overlook that possibility. But it is somehow profoundly comforting to believe that someone peered at Harriet's appeal, worked it out, and thought, "All right, why not?"

Having recently received a letter that was alarmingly addressed to "Lynne Truss, Her House, Brighton", I do worry that the Royal Mail may have too much of a sense of humour, actually. But that's another story. I do love this book. Each page is a little gift of ingenuity. In a country where mail is known as "post" I am bound to label Harriet as "post-modern"—but only in an ironic kind of way. I hope you enjoy this book. I made happy, yippy noises as I turned each page, mostly in appreciation of the light and lively spirit of the artist; but partly also at the ever-present notion of the downtrodden Scottish postal workers whose days were brightened by this clever stuff.

—*Lynne Truss*

PREFACE

While growing up, I had always been amused by the many odd spellings of the name of my house, Shulbrede Priory. There were so many variations—"Shrubdale", "Shellicole", "Shoebred", even "5 Hockle" and "Glenbroke"—that I found it amazing that the letters addressed as such actually reached our door. A collection made by my family of these envelopes with irregular spellings includes over 270 examples. I suppose the idea for the envelopes in this book really began with a fascination with this collection, and a desire to see how far the postal system could be challenged. I was also inspired by some decorated envelopes that my great-great-grandfather Henry Ponsonby (who was also Private Secretary to Queen Victoria) drew and painted, cleverly incorporating the address.

I began sending the envelopes, which I addressed to myself, in 1998, while living in Glasgow (of the 130 I sent, 120 arrived, and 75 of these appear in this book). The first few envelopes were very simple—I would write the address backward, indistinctly, or with words spelled very badly. At first glance, it is hard to imagine how most of the envelopes found their way back to me, as the addresses are so far removed from the conventional way of writing an address. However, they all have one important element—the postcode. I discovered that the main address could be totally indecipherable or incomplete, but if the postcode was displayed prominently there was a very good chance it would arrive, since only a small number of houses in the country ever share the same code.

I never actually spoke to our postman, but one of my flatmates did. When the postman asked where all the strange envelopes were coming from, I think my flatmate professed ignorance and explained that I was an art student. Anyway, although I never spoke to him or to any other postmen in Glasgow, I always got the impression that they rather enjoyed working out the puzzles. They started writing "solved by Glasgow mail centre" on the backs of the envelopes. I was amazed at their perseverance and willingness to involve themselves—one of the best examples of this is the crossword envelope. I sent this blank, and they worked out the clues and filled it in very neatly in red Biro. The postmen's annotations have become a real part of the work, adding an extra element that would not be there had they not participated.

I think they began to realise after a while that any strange-looking letter was likely to be for a certain flat in Montague Street (my Glasgow address). I started using other addresses as well—Shulbrede Priory in West Sussex, where my parents still live, and various friends' addresses, including one to my flatmate's parents in Devon whom I had not met at that stage and who must have got a rather odd first impression of me.

I tried to push things even further by writing addresses on Glaswegian train tickets and leaving them on the tube in London, in the hope that some kindly person would post one back to Glasgow for me. Most of these (of course) got lost, but about six months later, after I had moved out of the flat, one did arrive back, along with another ticket, a green, weekly London travelcard with the words "meet my fiancée." My Glaswegian ticket had found a friend!

Since leaving Glasgow, I have continued sending envelopes in London where I now live, and I have also sent envelopes from the United States.

The U.K. postal system has certainly exceeded my expectations. I am sure that the patience of many postmen has been severely tested by my unusual address writing, and I am extremely grateful to them and only hope that they were not too frustrated and confused by my envelopes.

A sincere thank-you to all those who have supported and encouraged this project over the last six years:

Mum, Dad, Panla, and Jo for their constant support and belief that the work would eventually see the light of day. All those friends who allowed me to use their address to send envelopes to, and who returned them to me: Andrew Dodds, Archi Quddus, Leanne Wylie, Miriam Elze, Paolo Marletta, and Mr and Mrs Hancock. Joe Hancock for his encouragement and ideas in the early days of the project. All at Central Illustration Agency in London, especially Louisa St. Pierre, who was instrumental in getting the project off the ground. All at Random House, especially Robbin Schiff for her hard work on my behalf and for being the one to finally say yes. Francine Rosenfeld and everyone at Bernstein and Andriulli, New York. Rosemary Davidson at Bloomsbury, and Mike Horseman at the Open Agency, who showed considerable support for the book. And Sophie Morrish, my tutor at Glasgow School of Art.

Finally, I'd like to thank the postal service in the U.K. and the U.S., as well as the Royal Mail. A special mention must go to the postal employees in Glasgow, especially the ones who delivered to 17 Montague Street. Without their dedication and hard work, this book would not exist.
—Harriet Russell

ENVELOPES

17

MONTAGUE

STREET

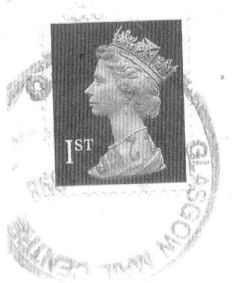

Please
Postmark
here→

Harriet Russell,
Flat 1/L,
17 Montague St.,
Woodlands,
Glasgow
G4 5HU

Flat Pencil Geese chicken stock Lenny Guitar Envelopes
Cher Phonebill 1/1 Bagels toast Fluff Mobile Portfolio Flat
1/1 Tea Easties lollipops YoYo Seventeen Training Academy Bikes
Cow tipping Seventeen Traffic Cone lightbulbs Henrietta Green
man Sofa Tinsel Christmas cake Montague Devon Times magazine
Mr MacDonald Tree Stirfry Royal Mail Infringements
section Montague street Safeway Virgil Hockey Soup
Earl Grey tea Seventeen Montague street, Flat 1/1
Sharp knives Scrabble Moscow Mule Bathroom
Woodlands scottish Power Art School sketchbook Charlie Pasta
Live TV. Post-it notes stamps Woodlands Simpsons Noodles
Bounce Corner shop Glasgow Yellow Vodka Green phone
Columns Sega Oblomov Tigger Cleopatra's Glasgow QM
Trash Tennis Toasties Dissertation Urinals Alcoholism Party
Memory loss Flat 1/1 Seventeen Montague street G4 9HU

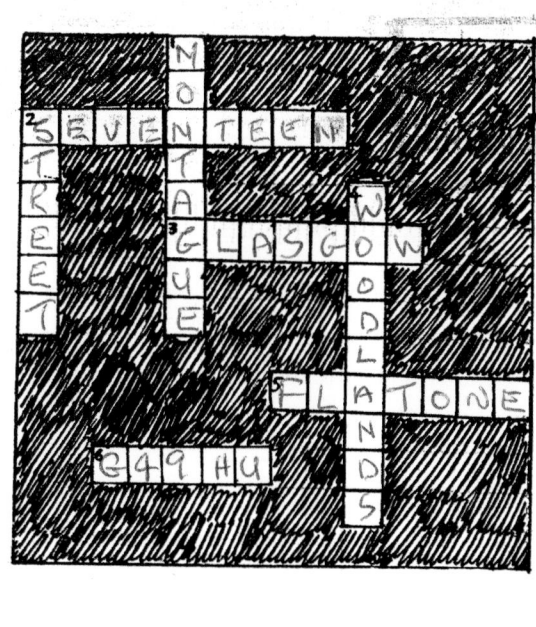

Across

2. 10 + 7
3. Scotland's largest city
5. Flat on the first floor, left.
6. Anagram: HUG49

Down

1. Romeo's surname
2. Public road in a town or village with houses on one or both sides.
4. Land with lots of trees on.

To Safeway

vegetable shop that sells Alligator steaks

corner shop that sells lots of porn mags

Lansdowne Cr.

GREAT WESTERN ROAD

KELVIN BRIDGE

Bank Street

Otago St.

Road

Montague St.

Holyrood Cr.

Burnbank Gardens.

Park

West

Barrington Dr.

Woodlands

Wood

Princes Street

WOODLANDS ROAD

The Hogshead

Oblomov, where we play scrabble

The Pink shop, where I have a developing relationship with the photocopier

Joe, Harriet & Tricia's flat
please deliver here
(Flat 1/1 Number 17)

1ST

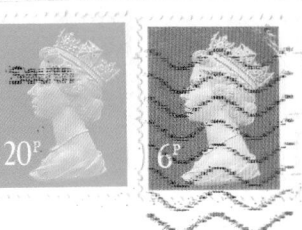

fl $\frac{}{}$ + at + (o.5 + o.5) =

20 + (I - 3) - I =

M (on) t+a+g (UE) + st =

W $\frac{00}{d}$ l (a+n) ds =

$\frac{G}{la}$ + S (go + w) =

G (29.2 -25.2) + 9hu =

G 2 a

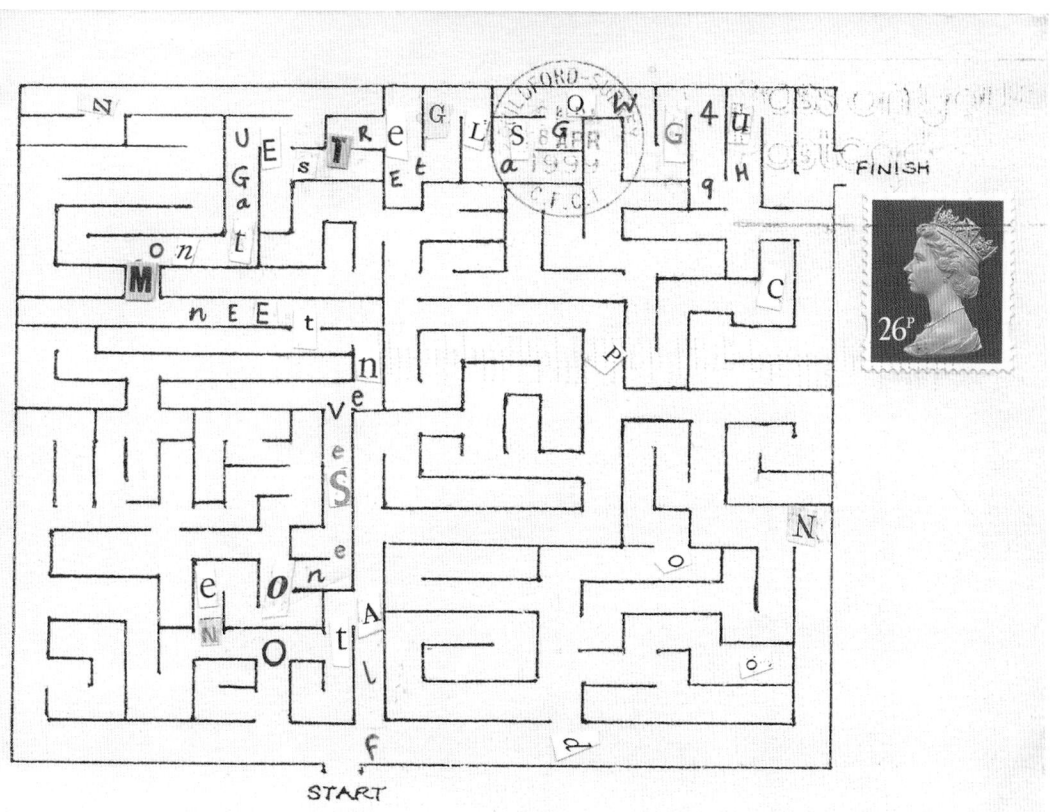

FINISH

START

· Dot to Dot ·

<u>*Menu (Priced at £7.95)*</u>

<u>*Starters*</u>

Tinned soup with sliced bread

Toast with blackcurrant jam

Flat first left

<u>*Main Courses*</u>

Pizza with ham and Pineapple

Chicken stir-fry with black bean sauce and noodles

Spaghetti bolognese (made with Safeway Savers spaghetti)

Seventeen Montague Street

Marmite and banana toasties

<u>*Desserts*</u>

Yoghurt (Assorted flavours)

Fresh (or not as the case may be) fruit

Glasgow

Tea (Earl Grey, Red Label, Nambarrie or de-caffinated)

Hot Chocolate

G4 9HU

- I'm goin' out
- Oh. Where ya goin'?
- Out
- Where ya goin' out?
- Dunno. Just out.
- Oh. Where ya goin' though?
- Dunno. Out. Just see what's goin' on. Know whattamean?
- Yeh
- D'ya wanna come out?
- Dunno. Depends. Where ya goin'?
- Out.
- Out.
- Out. Might be a party on.
- Yeh. Might be
- Where?
- Out
- Out where?
- Somewhere around. Here or there - see what's goin' on.
- Yeh. Think there's one in the West end.
- One what?
- Party. Dunno. Goin' out though
- Yeh.
- Think it's Montague street
- The Party?
- Yeh. Number 17. Think. Might not be though. Dunno.
- See what's going on.
- Yeah 17. Flat 1/1 might be. Yeah.
- Yeah. When d'ya wanna go then?
- Where?
- Out
- Out?
- Yeah. Out.
- Dunno. Might not go actually
- Nah
- Might stay in.
- In. Yeh. Friends is on.
- Might watch it. Might not.
- Yeh. Know what I mean?
- What ya do last night?
- Went out
- Did you? Where'd ya go?
- Out
- Oh.
- I'm bored of this conversation now
- So am I
- Let's go out
- Yeah. Where shall we go?

G4 9HU

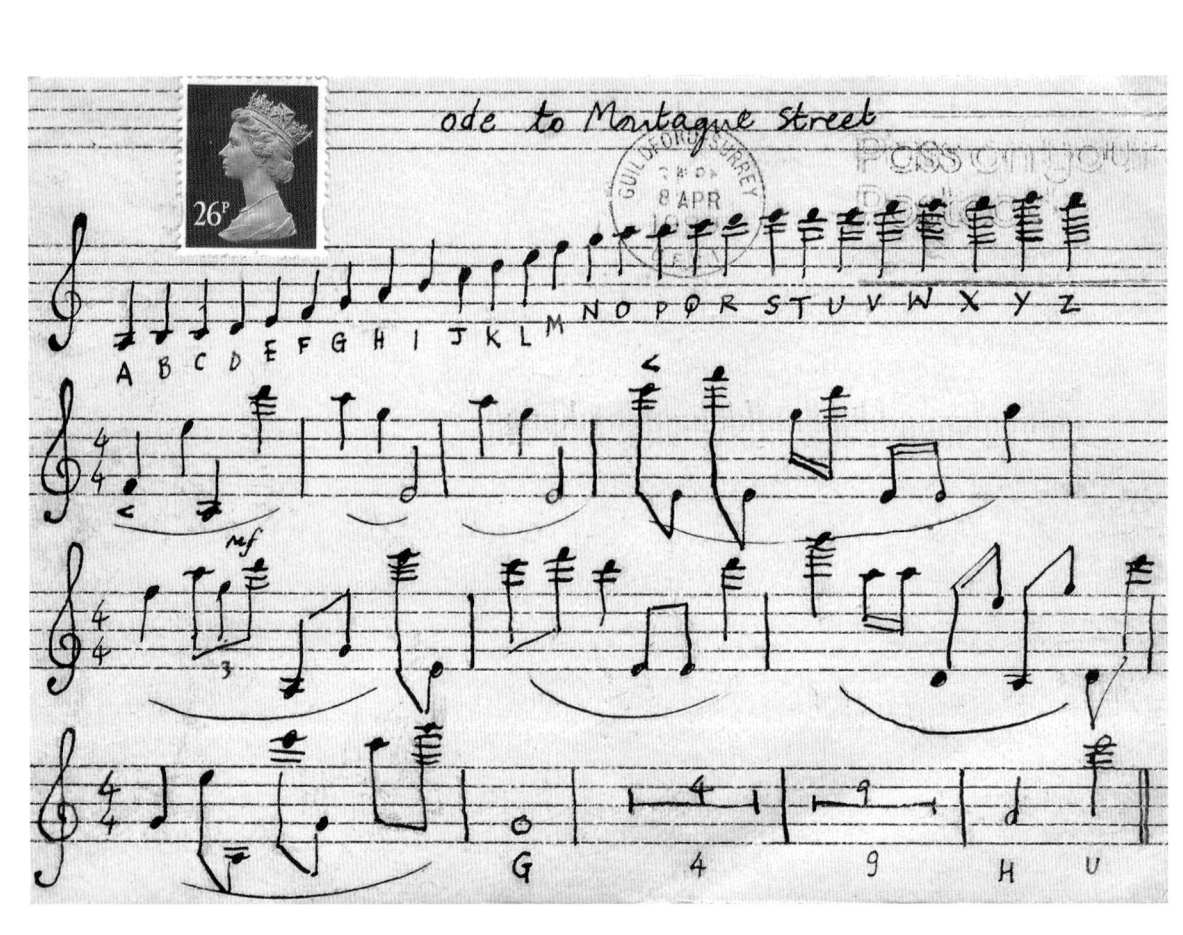

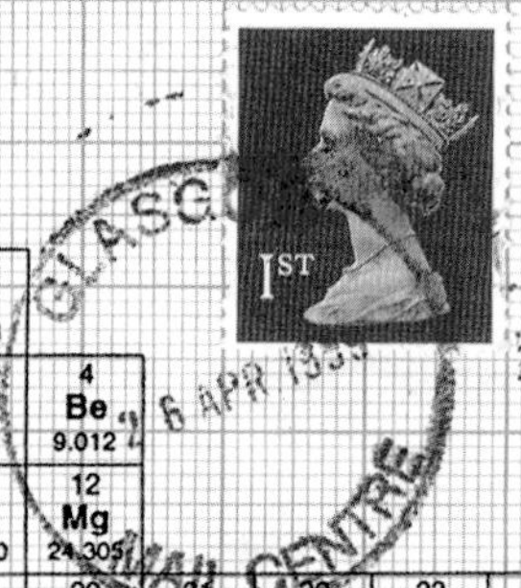

1 H 1.008																	
3 Li 6.941	4 Be 9.012																
11 Na 22.990	12 Mg 24.305																
19 K 39.098	20 Ca 40.078	21 Sc 44.956	22 Ti 47.88	23 V 50.942	24 Cr 51.996	25 Mn 54.938	26 Fe 55.847	27 Co 58.933	28 Ni 58.693	29 Cu 63.546	30 Zn 65.39						
37 Rb 85.468	38 Sr 87.62	39 Y 88.906	40 Zr 91.224	41 Nb 92.906	42 Mo	43 Tc (97.907)	44 Ru 101.07	45 Rh 102.906	46 Pd 106.42	47 Ag 107.868	48 Cd 112.411						
55 Cs 132.905	56 Ba 137.327	57–71	72 Hf 178.49	73 Ta 180.948	74 W	75 Re 186.207	76 Os 190.23	77 Ir 192.22	78 Pt 195.08	79 Au 196.967	80 Hg 200.59						
87 Fr (223.020)	88 Ra 226.025	89–103	104 Rf (261)	105 Db (262)	106 Sg (266)	107 Bh (262)	108 Hs (265)	109 Mt (266)	110 – (271)	111 – (272)	112 – (277)						

1 H 1.008	2 He 4.003
5 B 10.811	6 C 12.011	7 N 14.007	8 O	9 F	10 Ne 20.180
13 Al 26.982	14 Si 28.086	15 P 30.974	16 S	17 Cl 35.453	18 Ar 39.948
31 Ga	32 Ge 72.61	33 As 74.922	34 Se	35 Br 79.904	36 Kr 83.80
49 In 114.818	50 Sn 118.710	51 Sb 121.757	52 Te 127.60	53 I 126.904	54 Xe 131.29
81 Tl 204.383	82 Pb 207.2	83 Bi 208.980	84 Po (208.982)	85 At (209.987)	86 Rn (222.018)

57 La 138.906	58 Ce 140.115	59 Pr 140.908	60 Nd 144.24	61 Pm (144.917)	62 Sm 150.36	63 Eu 151.965	64 G4	65 Tb 158.925	66 Dy 162.50	67 Ho 164.93	68 Er 167.26	69 Tm 168.934	70 Yb 173.04	71 Lu 174.967
89 Ac 227.028	90 Th 232.038	91 Pa 231.036	92 U 238.029	93 Np 237.048	94 Pu (244.064)	95 Am (243.061)	96 Cm (247.070)	97 Bk (247.070)	98 Cf (251.080)	99 Es (252.083)	100 Fm (257.095)	101 Md (258.10)	102 No (259.101)	103 Lr (262.11)

Handwritten annotations within cells: "Glasgow" (Ga), "Seventeen" (As), "One" (O), "Flat" (F), "Street" (S), "Montague" (Mo), "Woodlands" (W), "9KV" (Eu).

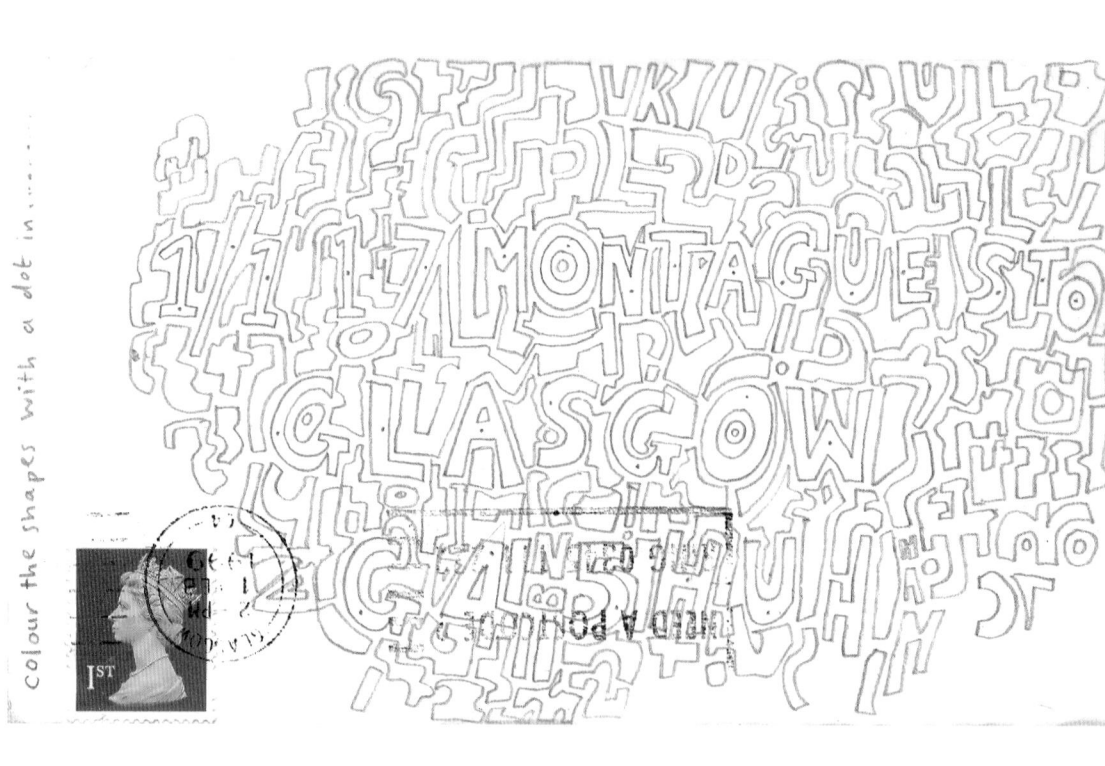

Colour the shapes with a dot in........

17 MONTAGUE ST G4 9HU
FLAT 1/1

Falcon Lampshade Armadillo
Topiary Ostrich Nasal Evergreen

Ostrich Nasal Evergreen,
Socks Evergreen Vacuum Evergreen
Nasal Topiary Evergreen Evergreen
Nasal Mosaic Ostrich Nasal
Topiary Armadillo Gingham Underground
Evergreen Socks Topiary Random
Evergreen Evergreen Topiary,
Woven, Ostrich Ostrich Damson Lampshade
Armadillo Nasal Damson Socks,
Gingham Lampshade Armadillo Socks
Gingham Ostrich Woven
Gingham 4 9 Hobnobs Underground

(Take the first letter of every
word)

Flat 1/1

17 Montague st.

10-02-08

G4 Glasgow

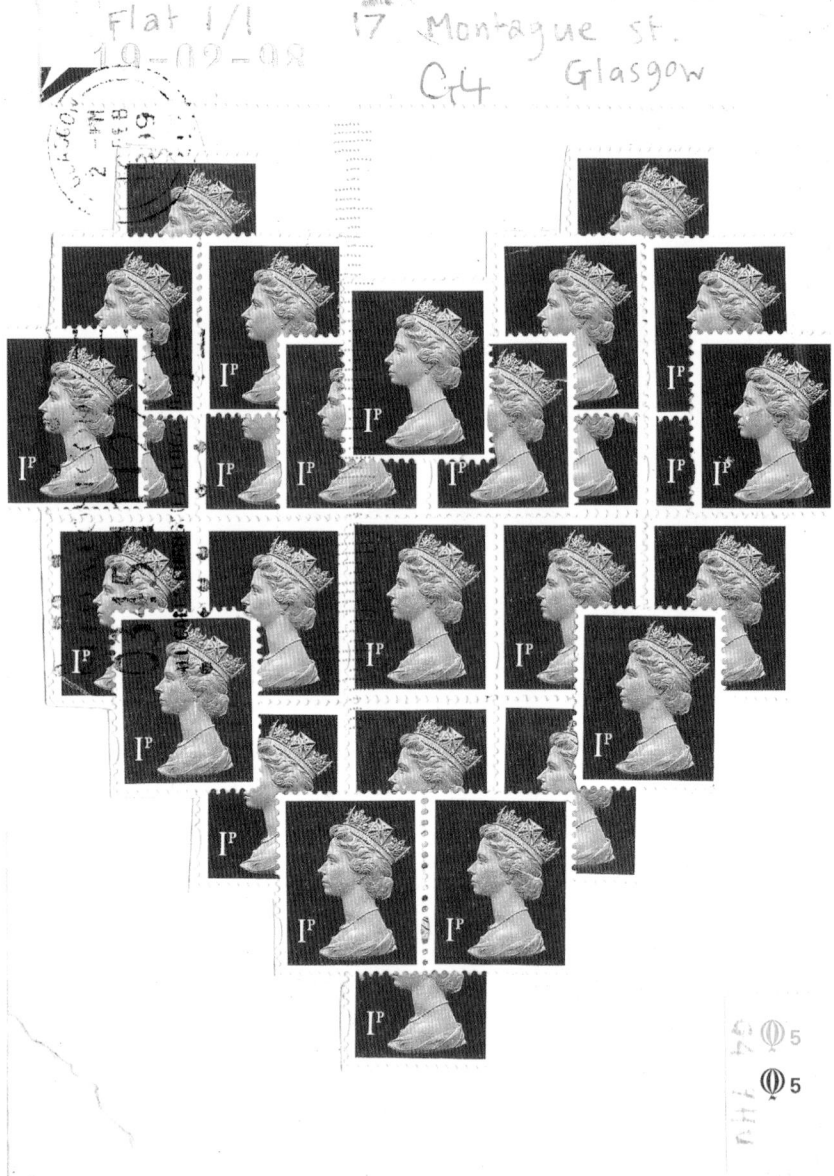

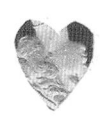

Harriet:

O gentle Flat 1/1!,
If though dost love, pronounce it faithfully:
Or if thou think'st I am too quickly won,
I'll frown, and be perverse, and say thee nay.
So thou wilt woo; but else, not for the world.
In truth, fair Seventeen Montague Street I am too fond,:
And therefore thou may'st think my havoiur light:
But trust me, Flat 1/1, I'll prove more true
Than those who have more cunning to be strange.
I should have been more strange, I must confess, although ,
You must admit, I am pretty strange already.
My true love's passion, Seventeen Montague Street:
* therefore pardon me;*
And not impute this yielding to light love ,
Which Woodlands, Glasgow hath so discovered.

17 Montague Street:

Lady, by yonder blessed moon I swear,
That tips with silver all these other flats -

Harriet:

I hear some noise within: dear love, adieu! —
Anon, Joe & Trish ! — Sweet Montague Street, be true.
Stay but a little, I will come again.
O blessed, blessed G4 9HU!

New Edition 1972

CHAMBERS TWENTIETH CENTURY DICTIONARY

Edited by A M Macdonald BA(Oxon)

owner
landlord

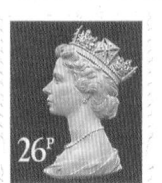

26ᴾ

See inside for address -(if you get
stuck look on back page)

(-dez). [r.]
one, *wun, adj.* single: of unit number: undivided:
the same: a certain: a single but not specified:
first.—*n.* the number unity: a symbol represent-
ing it: an individual thing or person: a thing

fāte, fär; mē, hûr (her); *mīne; mōte*

---

on: to outstrip,
o lose the thread,
o swiftly (*obs.*).—
p. stripped.—*n.* a
n piece of rolled
space in a news-
in pictures (**strip**
g, football, etc.—
which strips: a
p'ings, last milk
club, one which
rtists; **strip'-leaf,**
rip lighting, light-
cent tubes; **strip**
narrow strip of
i; **strip'-mine,** an
, an ionised atom
ctrons have been
ct of undressing
lace of entertain-
streifen; perh.

a lash: a band of
e, indicating non-
d behaviour: a

---

stroke, *strōk, n.* an act or mode of striking: a
hit or attempt at hitting: a blow: a striking
by lightning: a reverse: an attack of apoplexy
or of paralysis: the striking of a clock or its
sound: a dash or line: a touch of pen, pencil,
brush, etc.: a trait (*obs.*): a beat, pulse: a
single complete movement in a repeated series,
as in swimming, rowing, pumping, action of an
engine: a stroke-oar: a single action towards
an end: an effective action, feat, achievement.—
v.t. to put a stroke through or on: to cross
(commonly with *out*): to row stroke in or for:
to row at the rate of.—*v.i.* to row stroke.—
stroke'-oar, the aftmost oar in a boat: its rower
(also **stroke, strokes'man**), whose stroke leads the
rest. [O.E. (inferred) *strāc;* cf. Ger. *streich.*]
stroke, *strōk, v.t.* to rub gently in one direction:
to rub gently in kindness: to put by such a movement: to soothe, or flatter (*obs.*): to milk, strip:
to tool in small flutings: to whet: to set in close
gathers.—*n.* an act of stroking.—*ns.* strok'er;
strok'ing. [O.E. *strācian*—*strāc,* stroke (n.); cf.
Ger. *streichen,* to rub.]
stroke, *strōk,* stroken, *strōk'n,* obs. forms (*Spens.,*
Shak.) of struck. See strike.

(-dez). [r.]
one, *wun, adj.* single: of unit number: undivided:
the same: a certain: a single but not specified:
first.—*n.* the number unity: a symbol represent-
ing it: an individual thing or person: a thing

fāte, fär; mē, hûr (her); *mīne; mōte*

---

for Silesia between Frederick the Great and the
Empress Maria Theresa (1756-63). [O.E. *seofon;*
Du. *zeven,* Ger. *sieben,* Goth. *sibun,* Gr. *hepta,*
L. *septem.*]
seventeen, *sev-n-tĕn',* or *sev', n.* and *adj.* seven
and ten.—*adj.* sev'enteen-hund'er (*Burns*), woven
with a reed of 1700 divisions, i.e. fine linen.—
adj. and *n.* sev'enteenth (or *-tĕnth'*).—*adv.*
seventeenth'ly. [O.E. *seofontiene*—*seofon, tien,*

---

of St Augustine's mother; sometimes under-
stood as (Gr.) alone, solitary.
Montagu(e), *mon'tə-gū, m.* from the surname.—
Dim. **Monty.**

---

street, *strēt, n.* a paved road, esp. Roman (*ant.*): a
road lined with houses, broader than a lane, including or excluding the houses and the foot-
ways: those who live in a street or are on the
street: a passage or gap through or among any-
thing: brokers as a body: (often in *pl.*) prostitution.—*n.* street'age (*U.S.*), a toll for street
facilities.—*adj.* street'ed, having streets.—*n.*
street'ful:—*pl.* street'fuls.—*adv.* and *adj.* street'-
ward (*-ward*), towards or facing the street.—*adv.*
street'wards.—*adj.* street'y, savouring or charac-
teristic of the streets.—street'-Ar'ab (see Arab);
street'-boy, a boy who lives mainly on the street;
street'-car (*U.S.*), a tram-car; street'-door, the
door that opens on the street; street'-keeper, an
officer formerly employed to keep order in a
street or streets; street'-or'derly, a scavenger;
street'-rail'road, -rail'way, a town tramway.—
adj. street'-raking (*Scott*), ranging the streets.—
street'-room, space enough in the street; street'-
sweep'er, one who, or that which, sweeps the
streets clean; street'-walker, any one who walks
in the streets, esp. a whore.—*n.* and *adj.* street'-
walking.—street'-ward (*-wörd*), an officer who
formerly took care of the streets; streetway, the
roadway.—not in the same street as, much
inferior to; on the street (*slang*), homeless,
destitute; on the streets (*slang*), practising
prostitution; streets ahead of, far superior to;
up one's street (*fig.*), in the region in which one's
tastes, knowledge, abilities, lie. [O.E. *strǣt* (Du.
straat, Ger. *strasse,* It. *strada*)—L. *strāta* (*via*), a
paved (way), from *sternĕre, strātum,* to spread.]

HASLEMERE NATURAL HISTORY SOCIETY

FLORA OF BRITAIN

Botanical Name *Hamalis Russelliase*

Common Name *Harriet Russell*

Locality [17] *Montague Street, Glasgow (Flat 1/1)*

Habitat *Large room with horrible carpet in various shades of brown.*

Notes *lives on tea, pasta, stir fry and fajitas. Do not give her too much alcohol*

Date *Sept. '98*

Collector *Mr MacDonald*   Victim No. *17*

Anagrams :-

Alf. T -
Neo -
Neo -
Event Seen -
Age Mount -
T - Trees -
Wool dands -
Law Gogs -
HUG 94 -

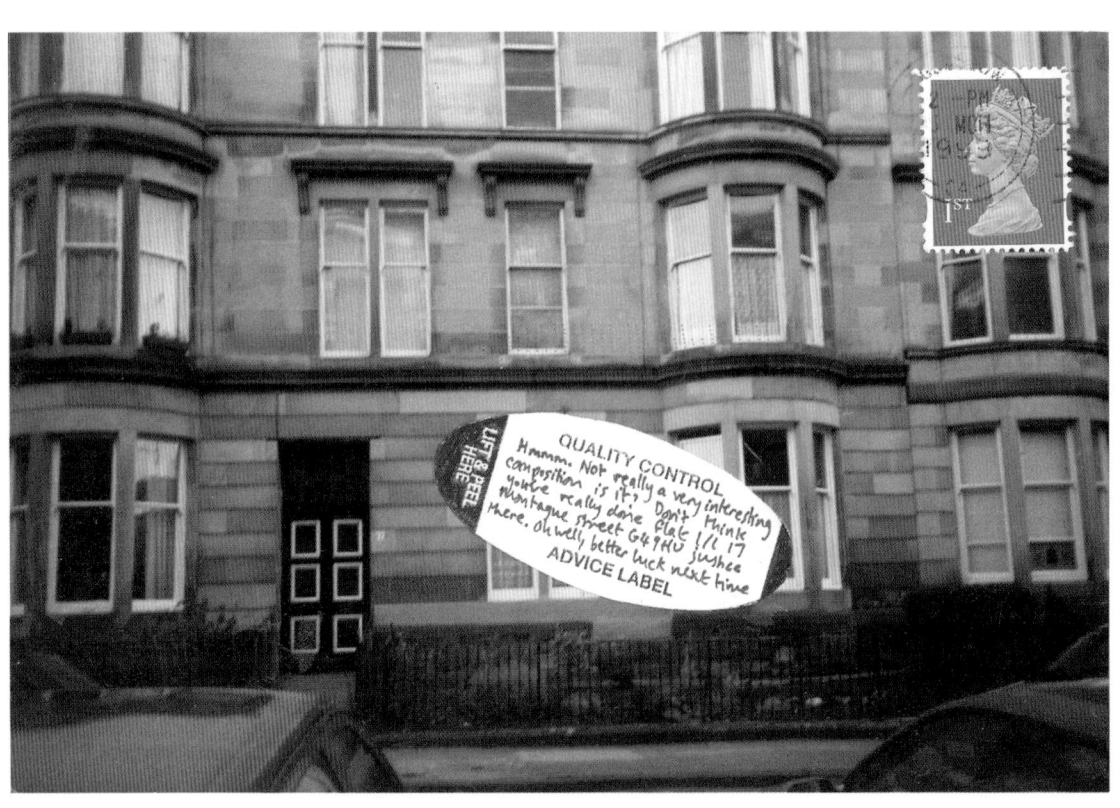

lat   e   teen   ag e tree   s

    on   street   s

at   e   Seven   e   a   r   s

    One   ag es

lat   e   r

at   Glasgow

                       G   o

to   Montague Street

                 n   ow

Flatoneoneseventeen Montague street Glasgow

Help. I'm a Glaswegian underground ticket loast oan the tube doon in London. It's big an scary an I cannae cope!

Please help me tae get back tae Glasgae noo by putting me in the nearest post box:- 17 Montague St, GLASGOW HB/ H37504 G4 9HU

Travelcard
Valid only when shown with photocard no. AG85150

Start date 29 SEP 99   Status   Ticket type 07DAY TRAVELCARI   Class STD

Expiry date 05 OCT 99   Zones »1234«

Meet my fiancée

Number 004 A375319 2123   Issue date 29SEP99 0729   Price £26.70

London Transport issued subject to conditions - see over

FLAT T/M
17 MONTAGUE ST
GLASGOW
G4 9AO

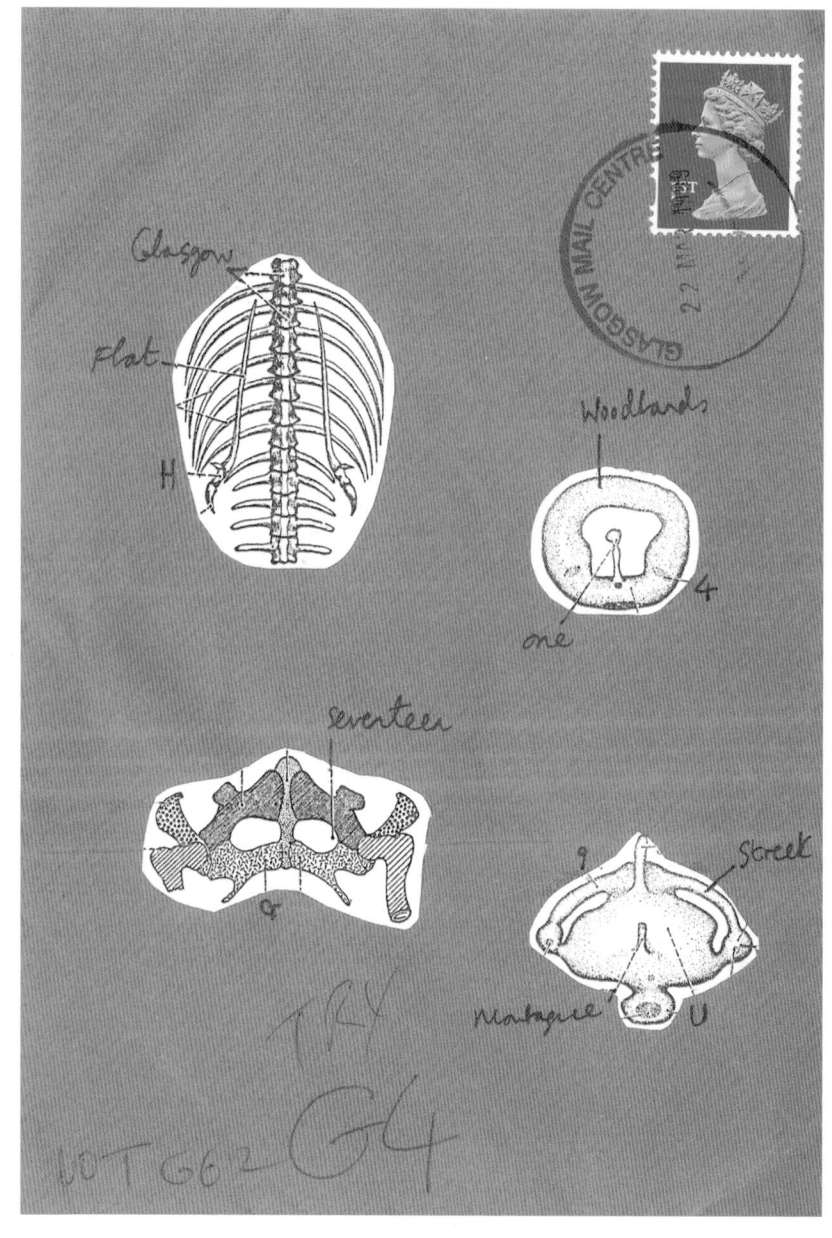

PLAN OF FLAT 1/1 17 MONTAGUE ST, GLASGOW G4 9HU.

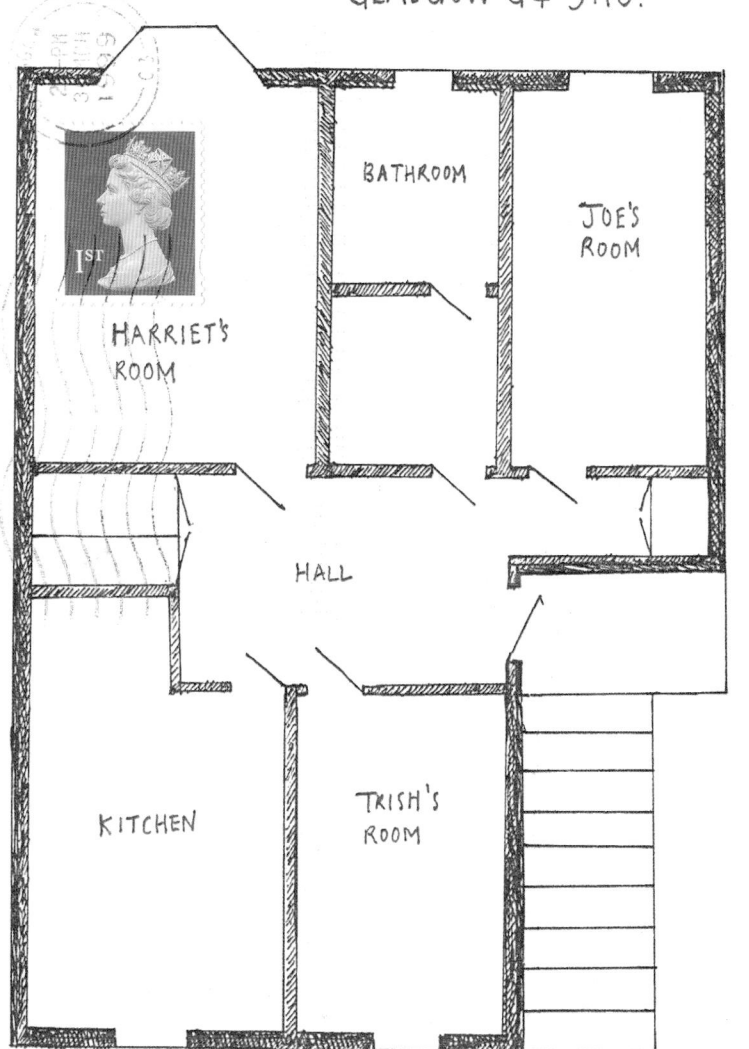

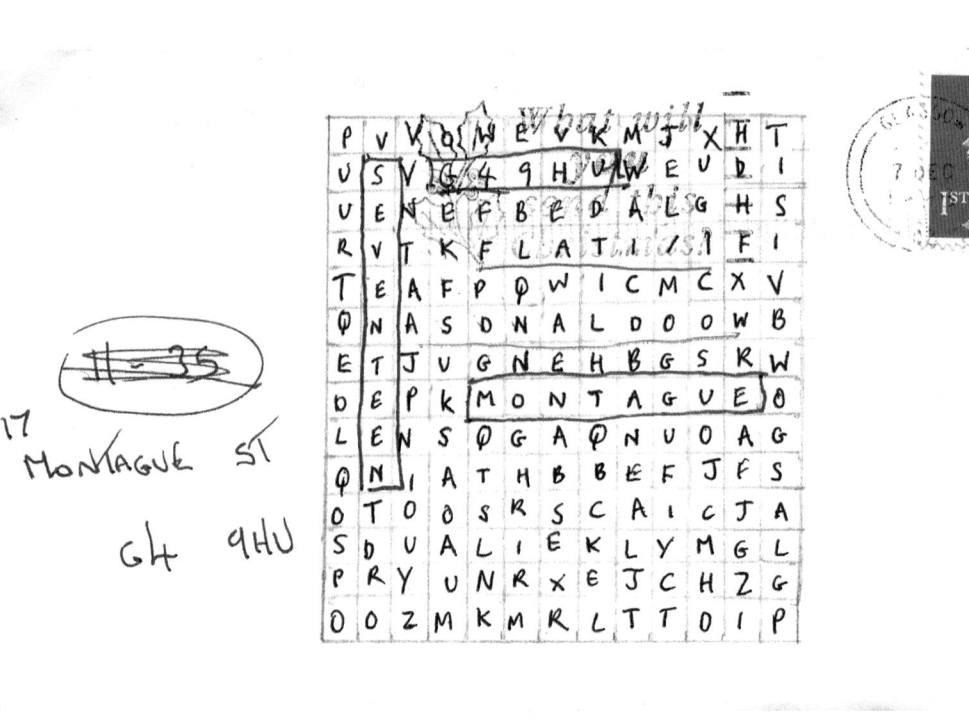

17
MONTAGUE ST
G4 9HU

WALL OF 17 MONTAGUE STREET

FLAT 1/1

SUNS AND MOONS AND SPACEY THINGS ON.

WINDOW OF JOE'S ROOM HE HAS CURTAINS WITH

WINDOW OF THE BATHROOM WE LIKE THE BATHROOM it's bright BLUE

WINDOW OF HARRIET'S ROOM HARRIET HAS BEIGE

CURTAINS, EVEN THOUGH SHE THINKS BEIGE

IS RATHER A BORING COLOUR IT WASN'T her choice, Anyway.

FRONT DOOR, BLACK, WITH white edged PANELS

17

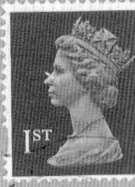

1ST

Stamp where window should be

WINDOW WINDOW WIN DOW

WIN DOW WIN DOW

WIN DOW WINDOW WIN DOW

G4 9 H U

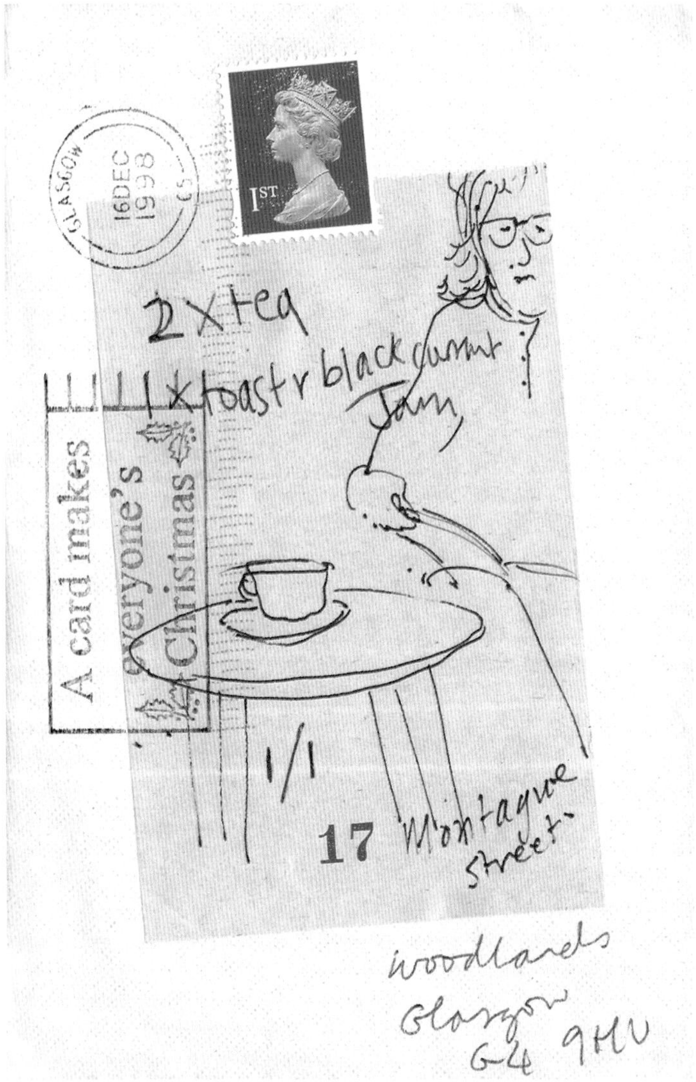

2 × tea
1 × toast + black currant Jam

A card makes
everyone's Christmas

1/1

17 Montague Street

Woodlands
Glasgow
G4 9HU

1ST

GLASGOW 16 DEC 1998

Oh no! It's
Valentine's Day

No it's
not!

It is - You're just
in denial because
you think you're not
going to get any
cards..

I'm not. I'm
a post it note.

Oh.

I'm telling you - it's
not Valentines day -
Valentine's Day's on a
Sunday + there's no post
on a Sunday - therefore
it can't be Valentine's
day.

O.K well it's
Valentines day
tomorrow or
yesterday - depending
on what day we arrive

Arrive?
What do you
mean?
Arrive where?

17 Montague
Street of course -
that's where all the
strange envelopes go.

Not....?

Yes... Flat 1/1
17 Montague street
Glasgow
G4 9HU

Oh
Good'
I
can't
wait

11 2 FEB 1999
1ST

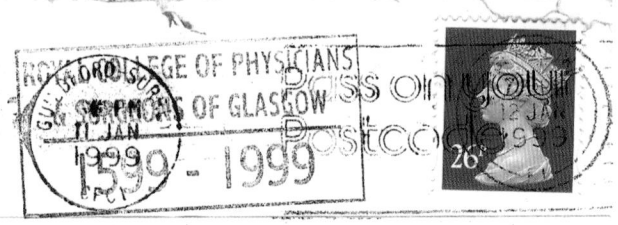

Old MacDonald had a flat,
Ee-I Ee-I Oh,
And that flat was at 1\1 17 Montague Street,
               (Glasgow G4 5HU),
Ee-I Ee-I Oh,
With a "JOSEPH!! Let me show you this" here and a "TRICIA! Stop your partying!" there,
Here a sharp knife, there a sharp knife, everywhere a sharp knife,

Legend has it that Praxiteles' statue of Aphrodite was so lifelike that a man tried to make love to it. One may have the impulse to lie down on a Gober bed, or to urinate in a Gober urinal, but with their pristine, fragile presence, and in the obvious care that went into their making, these objects are as divorced from functional objects as Praxiteles' statue was from living flesh. (In any case, the sinks have no faucets; the drains would void into the room.) The common ground between functional property and intellectual property (the terrain originally mapped out by the readymade) is really the least compelling element of Gober's work. His objects are made from memory rather than by a casting process or some other means of exactly duplicating an existing model; thus the sink pieces, for example, are better described as sculptures that look like sinks than as actual representations.

This helps to free up their metaphoric potential. The sink is an emblem of cleanliness, or of the effort to be clean. That prosaic association can easily be extended into a religious symbolism of purification, perhaps of atonement, a suggestion reinforced by the sculptures' whiteness, their absence of color, with its accompanying implications of innocence, of purity (surely a debunked aspiration in our age), or of deathliness. The latter reference works on both the personal and the social scale. Like the urinal, the sink is an agent of disappearance: where does the waste go? Implicit in these works, I suggest, is a poetic correlative for our society's habits of consumption, at the expense of the environment in which we live. But

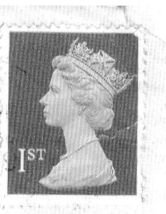

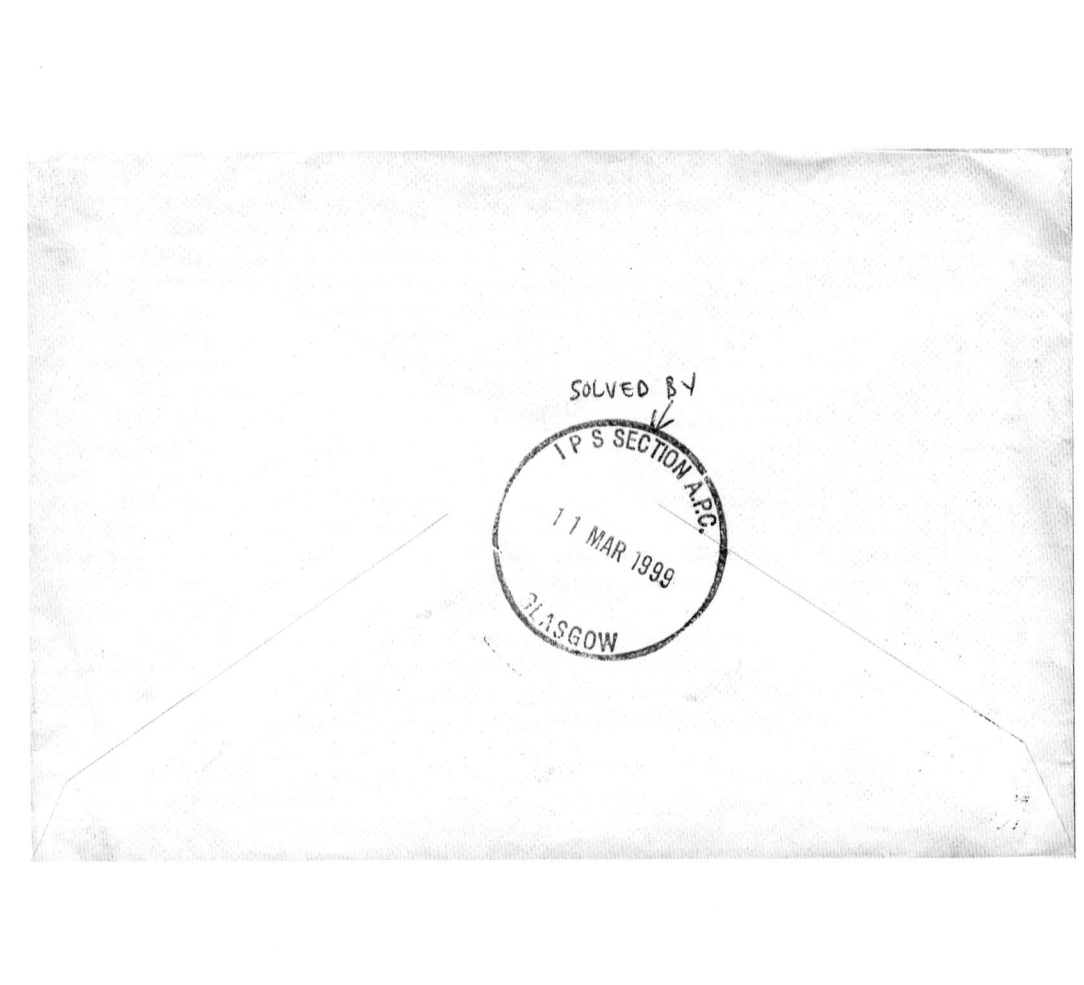

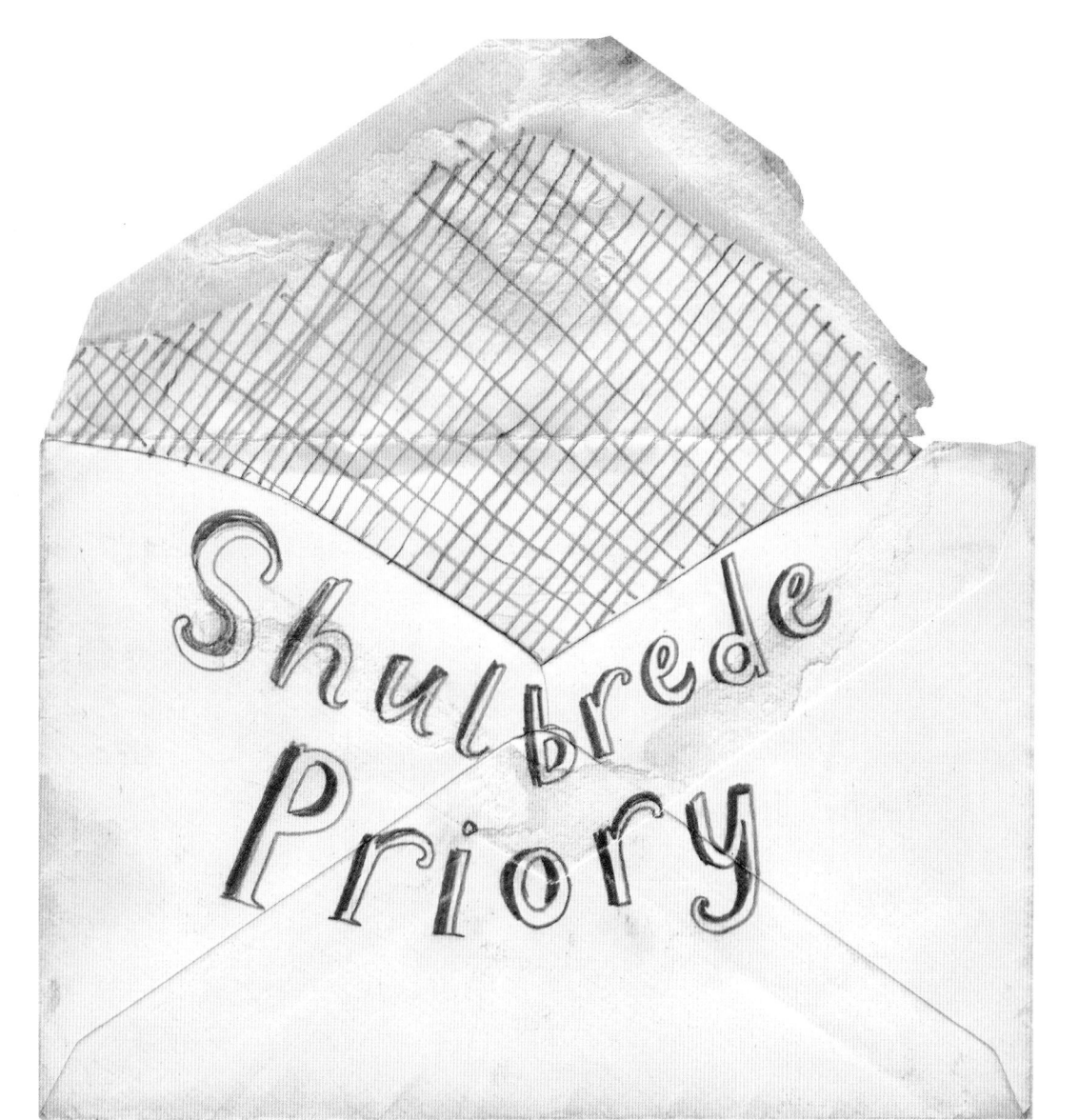

```
Shulbrede  Priory  Linchmere   Haslemere   Surrey
Shall breed Proiry  Lynchmere   Hazlemere   Surrey
Shoal bred  Parry   Lunchmere   Hazelmeer   Sorry
Shell bread Puree   Links more  Hassle more Curry
Shawl bird  Prairie Lunch here  Nasal here  Sherry
Ghoul brid  Primary Lank mare   Razor mare  Hurry
School bid   Dairy  Lench mar   Teazle mar  Harry
Cool bead   Pourri  Trench ere  Hazy mere   Carry
Call Bed    Party   Finch fear  Hazzle fear Furry
Crawl bad   Perry   Flinch dear Lazy dear   Marry
Scrawl bud  Fairy   Crunch Ma   Hasty Ma    Starry
Scroll bard Pansy   Lacks more  Hacks more  Ferry
Scale band  Potty   Larks tear  Dazzle tear Flutty
Sscore brode Polly  Wench leer  Hench leer  Tarry
Shore bride Pretty  Lance beer  Haggel beer Tarty
```

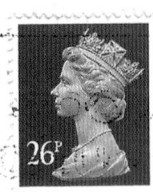  26P

GU27 3NO

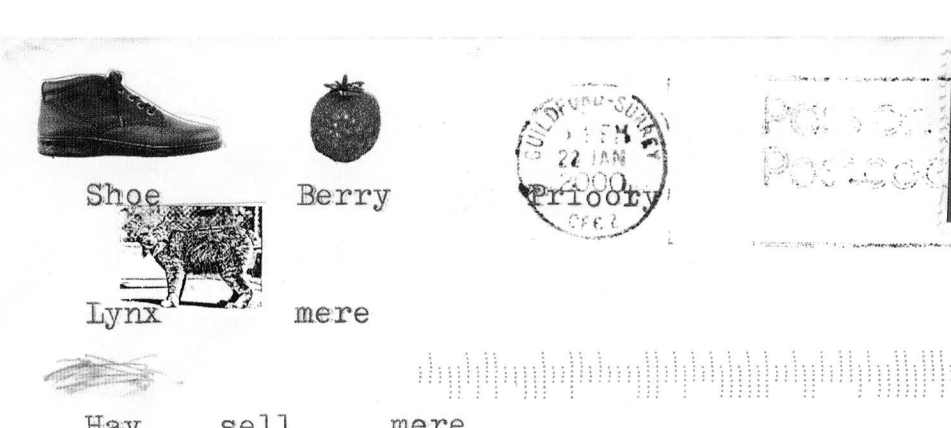

Shoe   Berry

Lynx   mere

Hay   sell   mere

Scurry

GU27 3NQ

Priooly

22 JAN 2000

26ᴾ

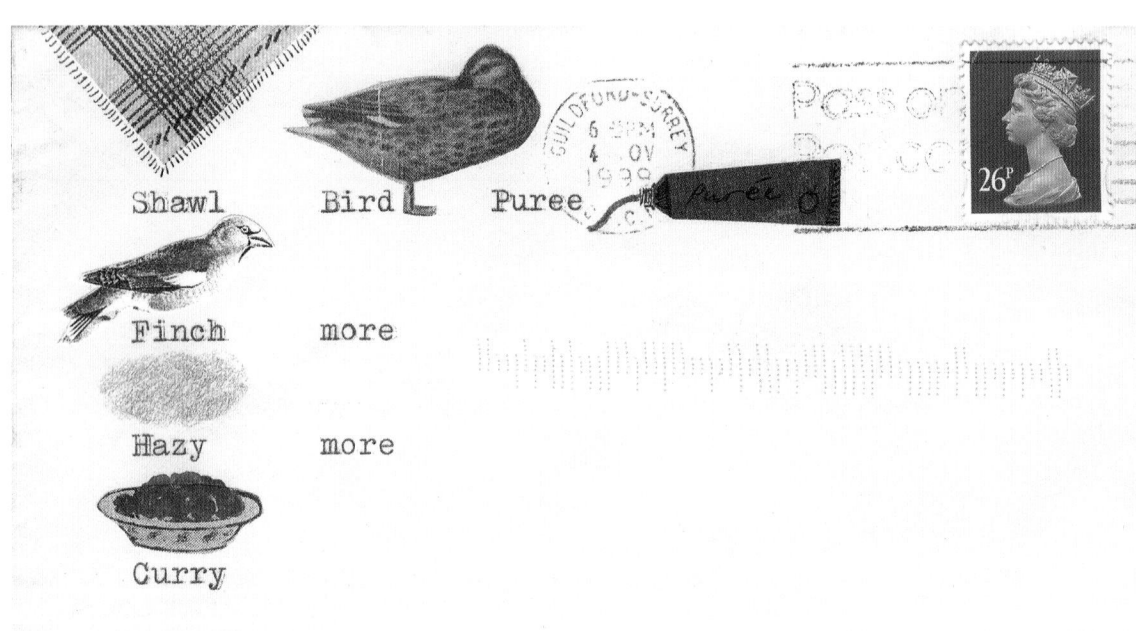

Shawl   Bird   Puree

Finch   more

Hazy   more

Curry

GU27 3NQ

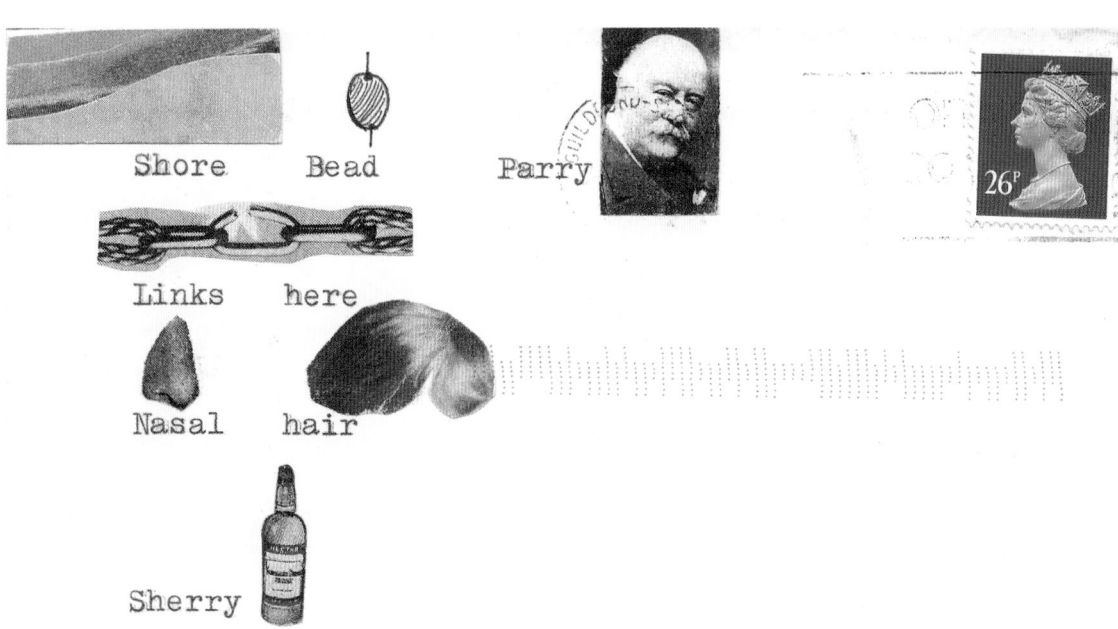

Shore   Bead   Parry

Links   here

Nasal   hair

Sherry

GU27 3NQ

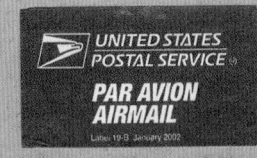

80

US NEW YORK NY
OCT
2014
P.
100

DO NOT BEND

DO NOT spill your coffee over

DO NOT tear up or damage in any way

DO NOT put on one side to deal with later

DO NOT BE nasty

DO NOT END the day on an argument

DO   BE happy

DO   END sentences with a full stop

DO   BEND bendy straws

DO deliver to: Shulbrede Priory, Linchmere,

Haslemere, Surrey, GU27 3ND England U.K.

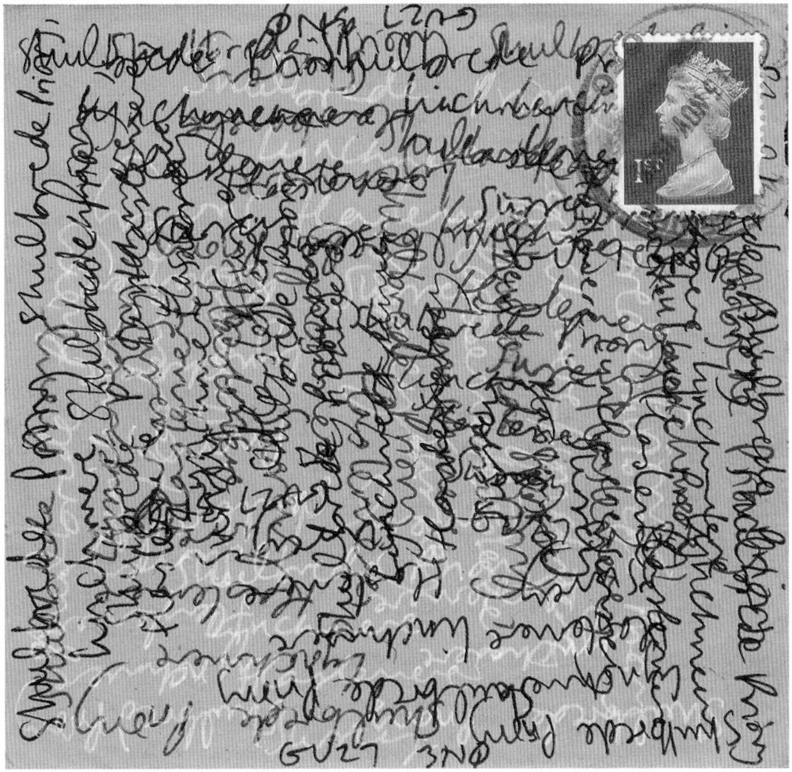

Shopping List

- Tinned tomatoes x 2
- Potatoes (1 bag)
- Onions
- Shulbrede Priory
- 1lb Carrots
- 1pkt Cinnamon Bagels
- Linchmere
- Crumpets
- Milk (Semi-Skimmed)
- Haslemere
- 1lb Beef Mince
- Lasagne
- Surrey

- Breakfast
- Cornflakes
- 6oz mature cheddar
- Cooscous
- Pasta (loose)
- GU27 3NQ
- lollipops

What will you send this Christmas?

GU27 3NQ   No. I   (Shulbrede Priory)

Go
Up to the
2nd floor
7th room on the left

And you'll see3
        N ice - looking
        Quail

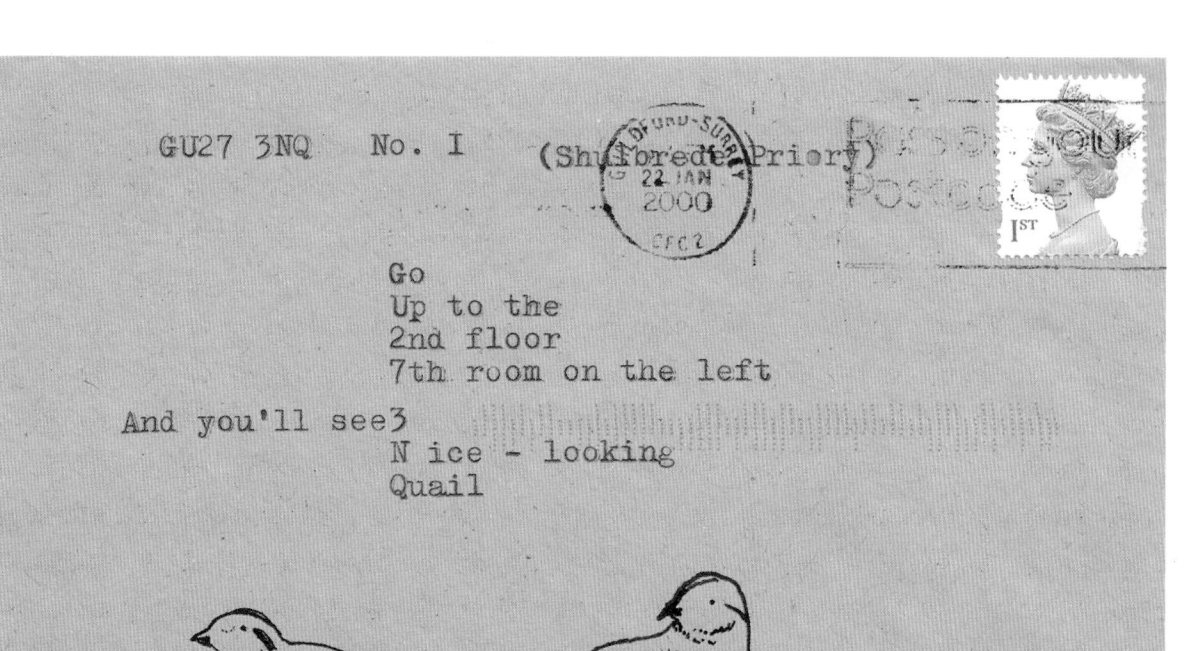

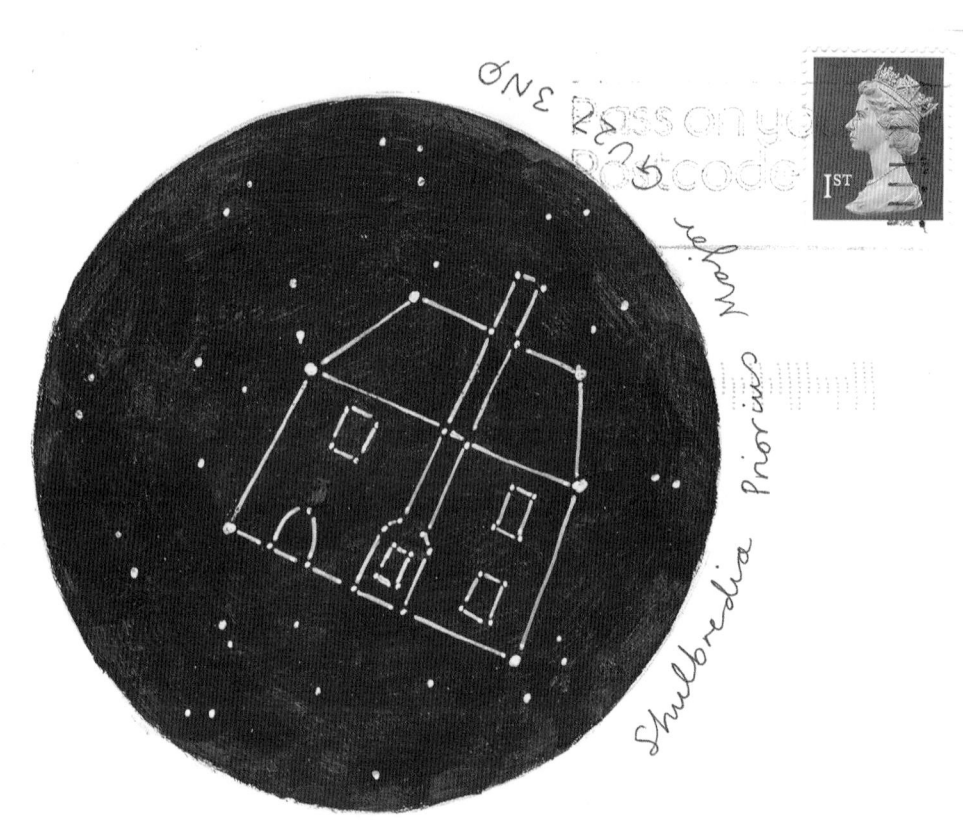

Shrilbrede

STRULBREDE PRIORY

Shellwood Priory

Schoolbury Priory

Shaudbrede Priory

Shudgrove Priory

"Shoolbrede Priory

Shulbreda Priory

Shullwell Priory.

Shalbrode

Shullwell Priory

Shribbe d Priau

Schulebride Priory

SHERLBRIDGE PRIORY.

Shulbrede Priory

Shelwell Priory

Schoolbrede Priory

Shelfredt Priory

Shalbrede Priory

Schulbredd Priory

1ST

GUILDFORD-SURREY 6 PM 11 NOV 1999

GU27 3NP

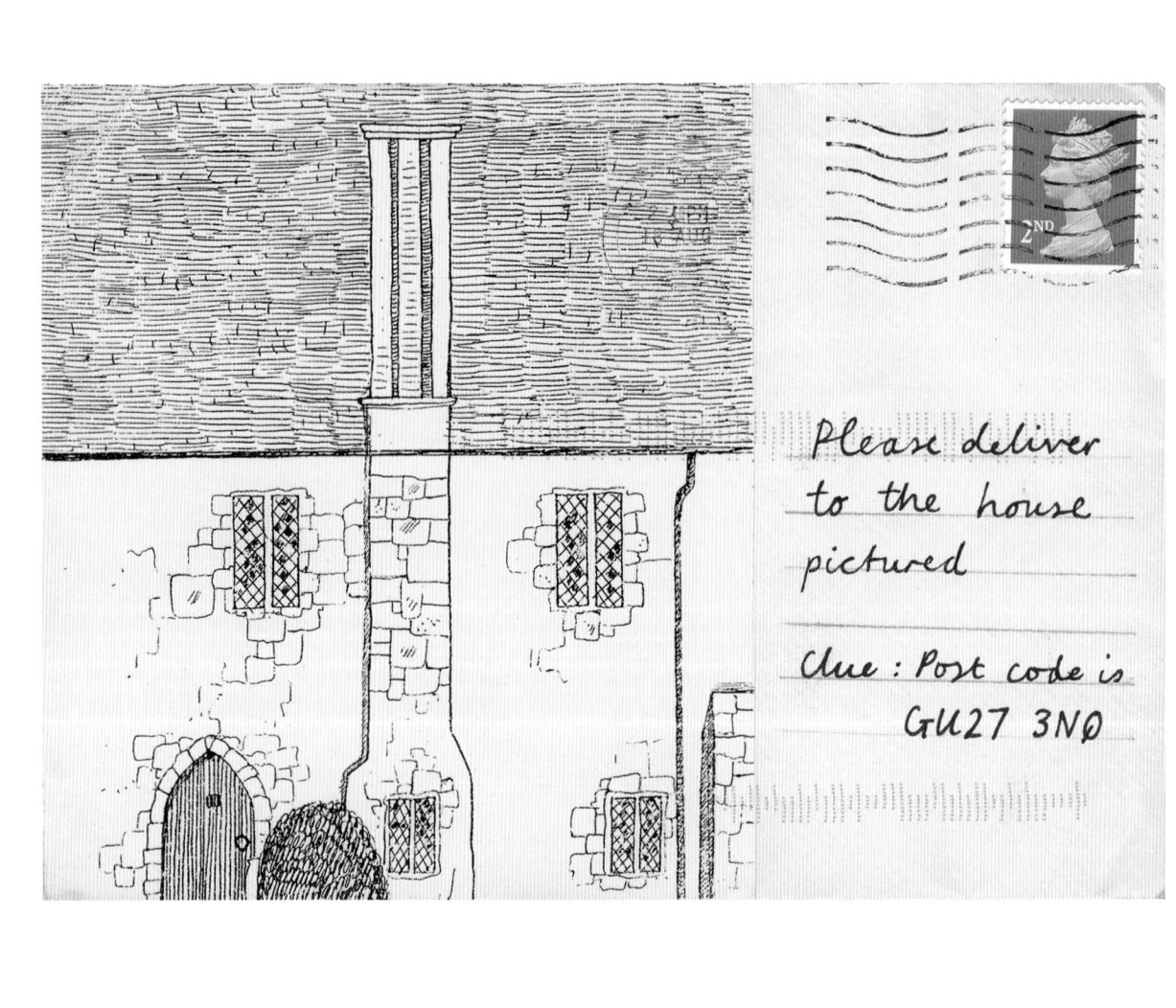

Please deliver
to the house
pictured

Clue : Post code is
GU27 3NQ

Hello. I am an envelope. I haven't had much of a life so far. After I was born I was delivered with a lot of other brown envelopes to a shop called John Menzies in Glasgow where I sat on a shelf and looked at various people who were passing by. It was very uncomfortable because I was squashed between many other brown envelopes who were on either side of me. After several days of sitting on a shelf I was picked up and examined by an old lady. My heart leaped - perhaps I could leave the shelf at last? However, it was not to be; and the old lady shook her head & put me down, saying 'ooh no, I was really looking for something a little bigger,' and white would be better.' I could scarcely hide my disappointment. So, I'm not big enough and I'm not white.? I really think this sort of discrimination is unfair. I sat on the shelf in a bad mood for a few days ..... and then ... at last a girl called Harriet came along, took me right off the shelf, and put me on a counter, and then into a very dark, sack like thing. I stayed there for a few hours, and was jolted about a bit. Then, at last, I was taken out and put on a wooden thing. I didn't have much to do for a whole day or so because Harriet was busy with other things like painting her kitchen. However, then, she decided to send me on a trip to the South of England. She licked an orange thing with a picture of a woman on it and stuck it to me. Then she wrote down where she wants me to go:

Shulbrede Priory,
Lynchmere,
Haslemere,
Surrey
GU27 3NQ

I leave tomorrow and I'm looking forward to it very much. I I do hope I get there all right.

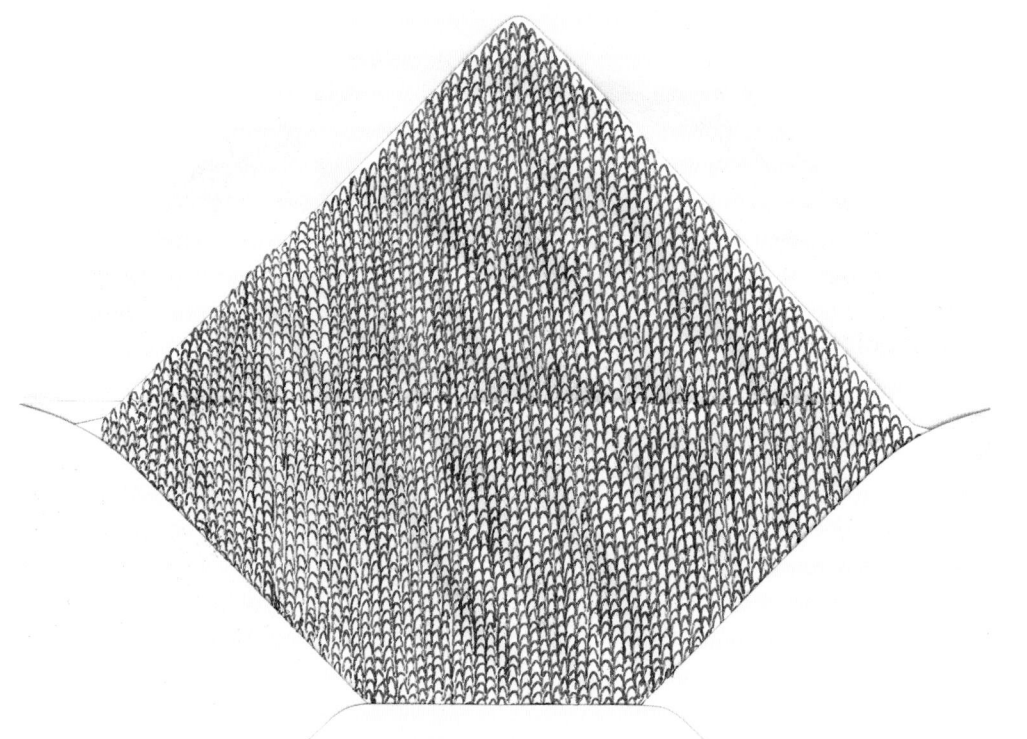

175
Sussex
Gardens

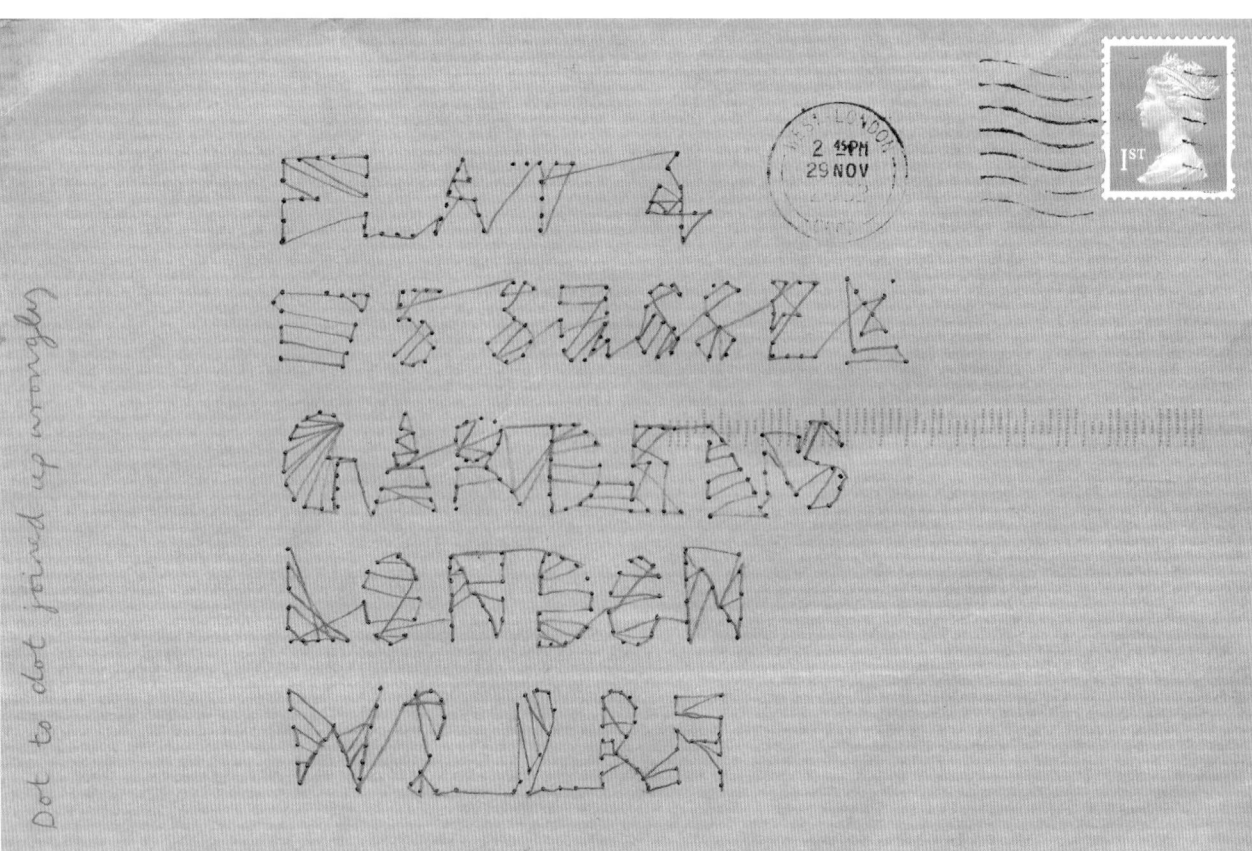

FLAT 4
75 SUSSEX
GARDENS
LONDON
W2 1RL

Dot to dot joined up wrongly

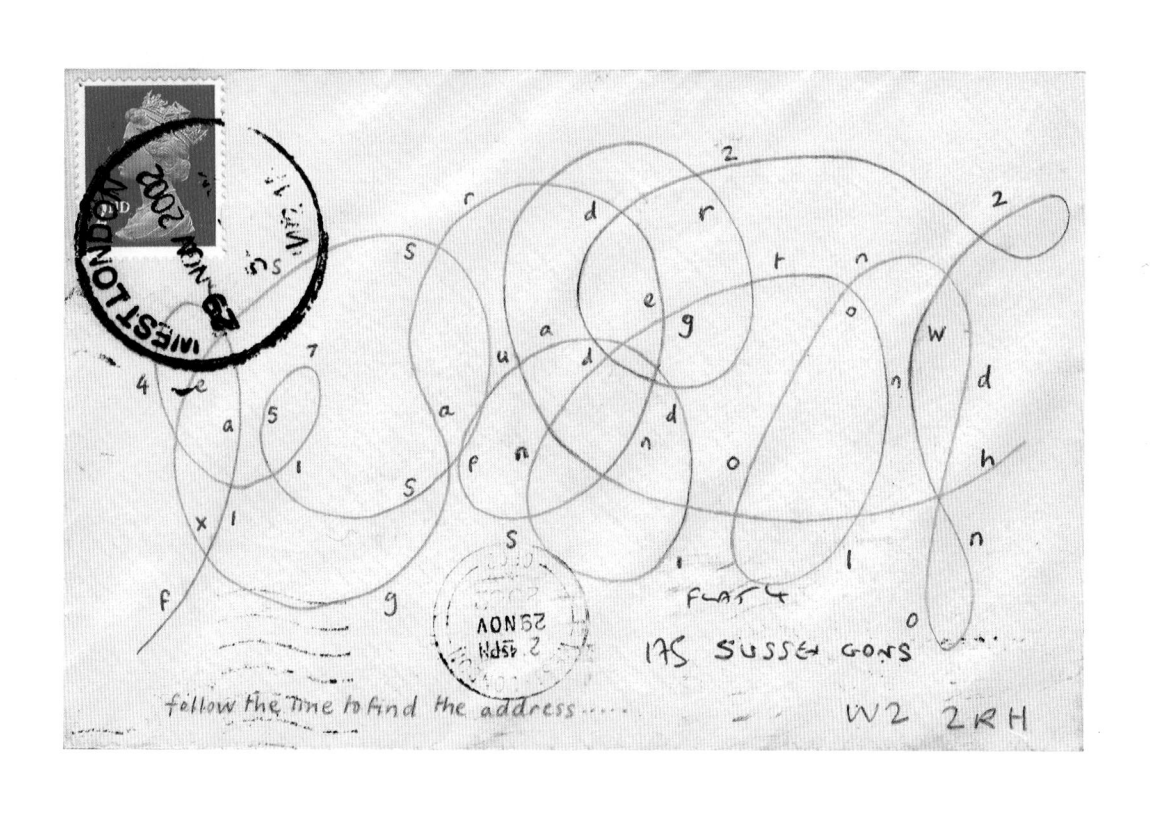

follow the line to find the address.....

FLAT
175 SUSSEX GDNS
W2 2RH

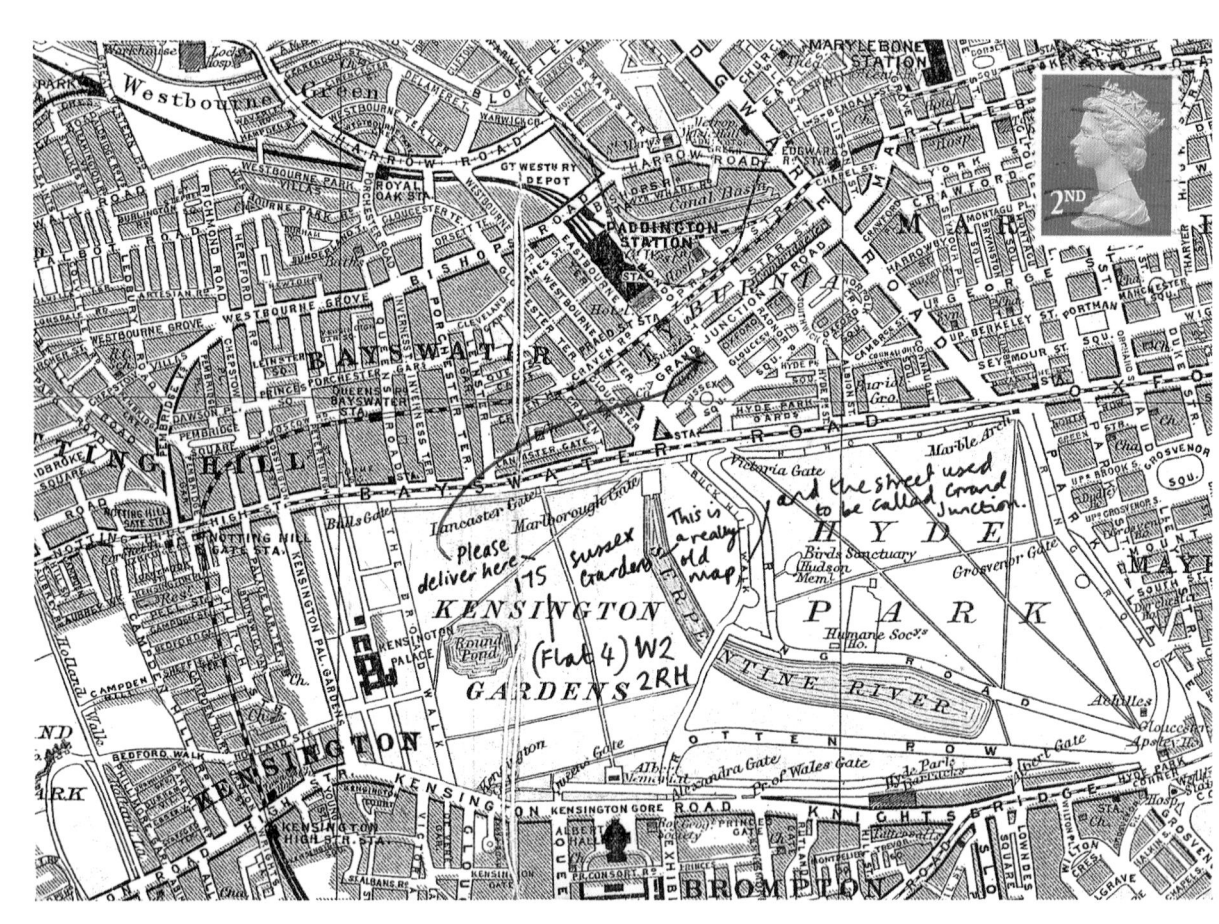

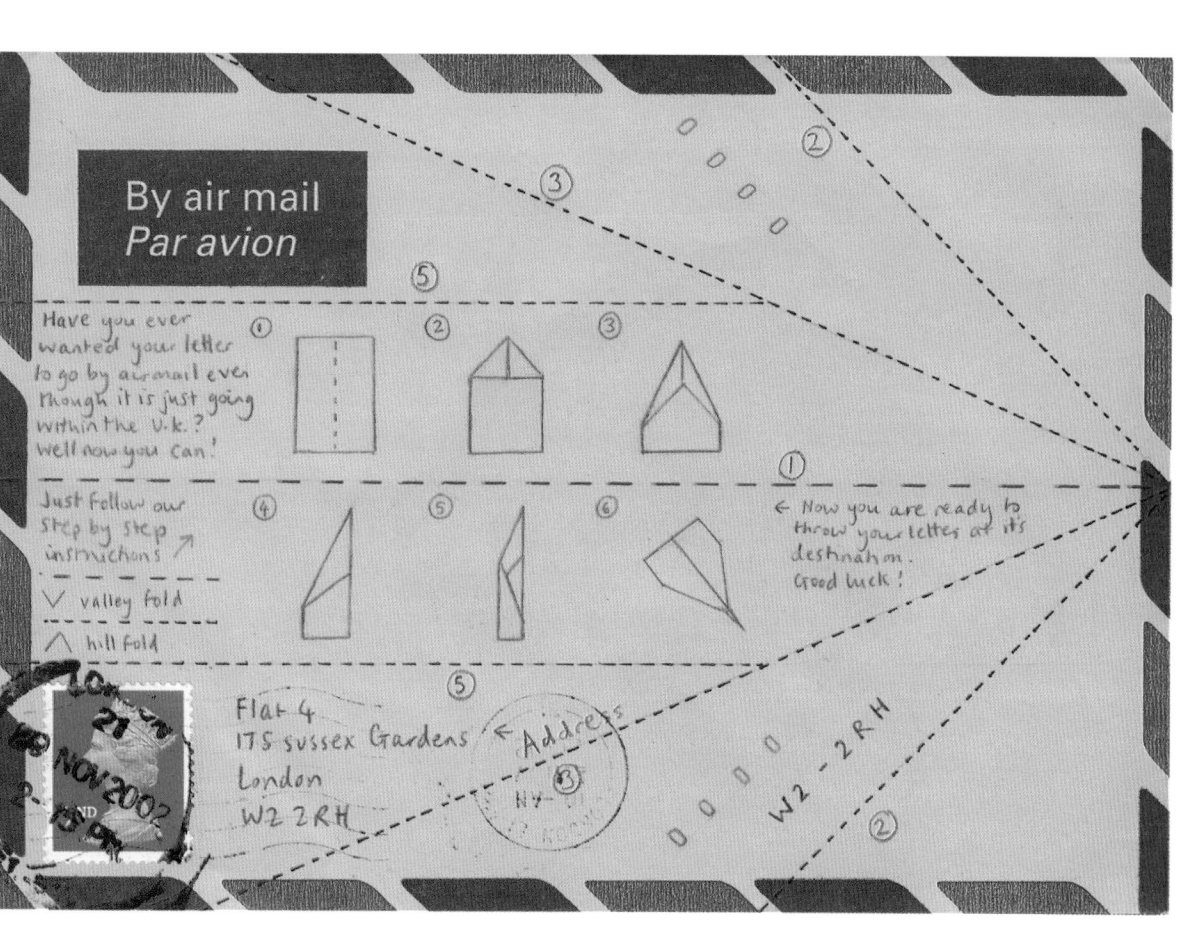

colour blindness test.....

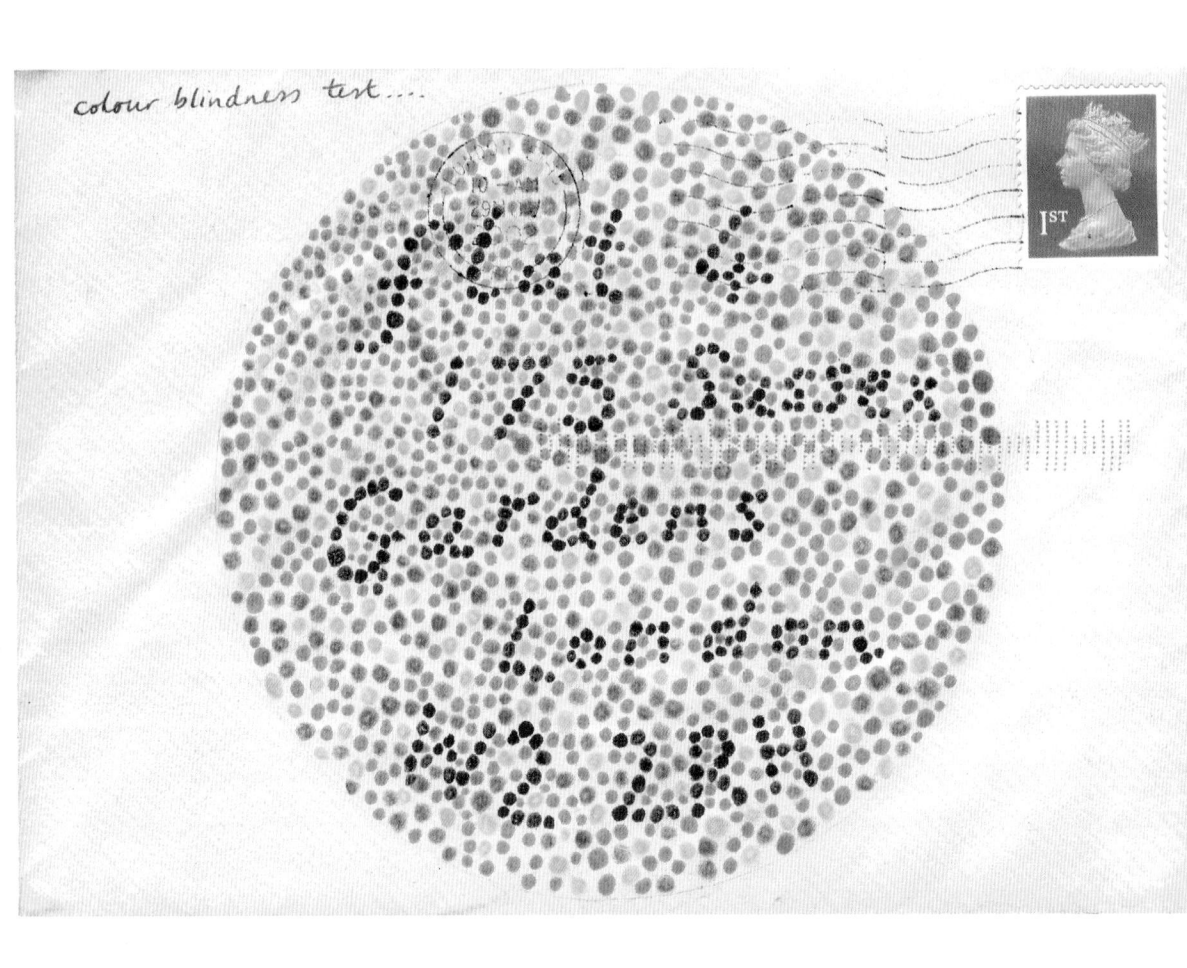

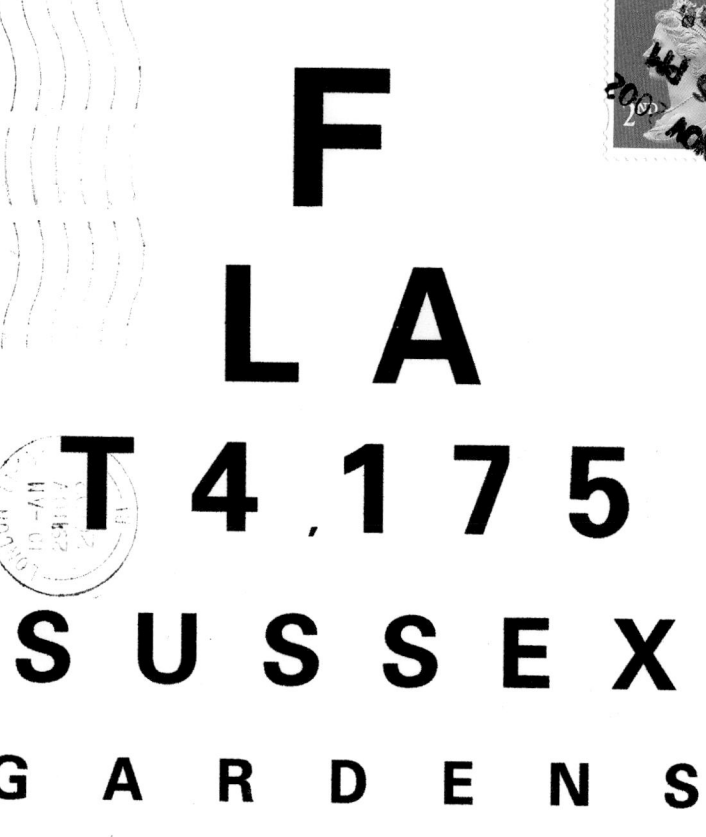

eye chart.

RUSSELL/HA
ENVELOPE (01)
TO

SSX GDNS

LONDON
W2

2R H175 (4) SEP 04

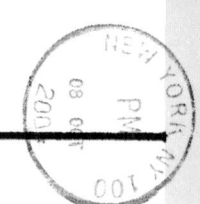

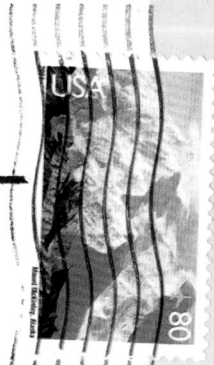

0000207544

BY AIR MAIL
par avion
Royal Mail

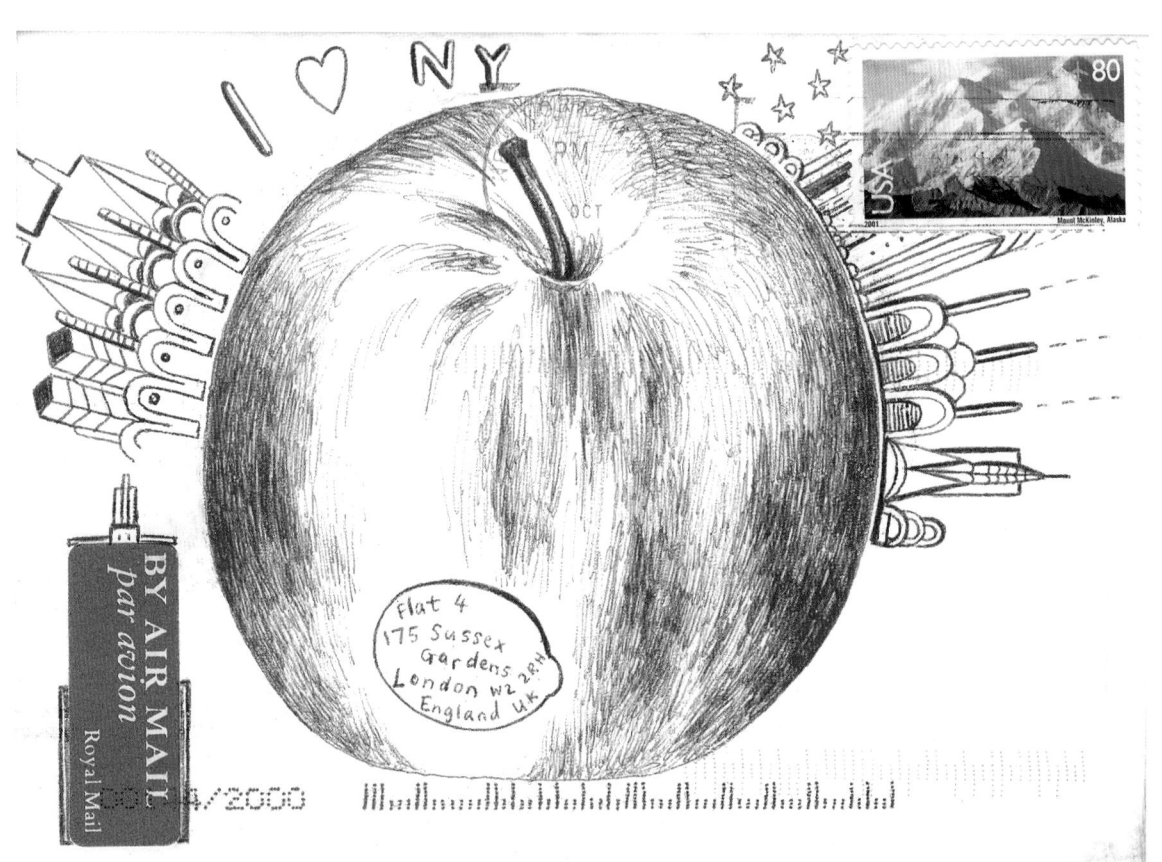

Fish fingers
laddered tights
ankle socks
tea bags (earl grey)

Fags (Jason's)
orange blanket
umbrella
rock
old chocolate
now 12 tape
elephants (not live)

skeleton costume
eggs
videos (pretty limited collection inc. Beverly Callard work-out
end of a loaf of bread (probably mouldy)
nougat (unopened, several years old)

fairy lights in a bowl
inflatable chair
vase
elderly A-Z (circa 1970)
sean the sheep timer
underwear (various)
spice girls Cd (not mine)
shower gel
eggs
xerox copies
grater

armadillo (not really)
ready-brek
devil horns (flashing)
empty bottles
nail scissors
stripey scarf
lots of very similar camel coloured coats
out of date milk
nonsense books

dust
oven gloves
noodles

washing rack that keeps falling apart
things for holding the washing rack together
wing nuts
oxo cubes

t.v with unusually crap reception
water filter
oyster sauce

rugs
hot water bottle   4175

WR 2RH

(Address in red, reading downwards)

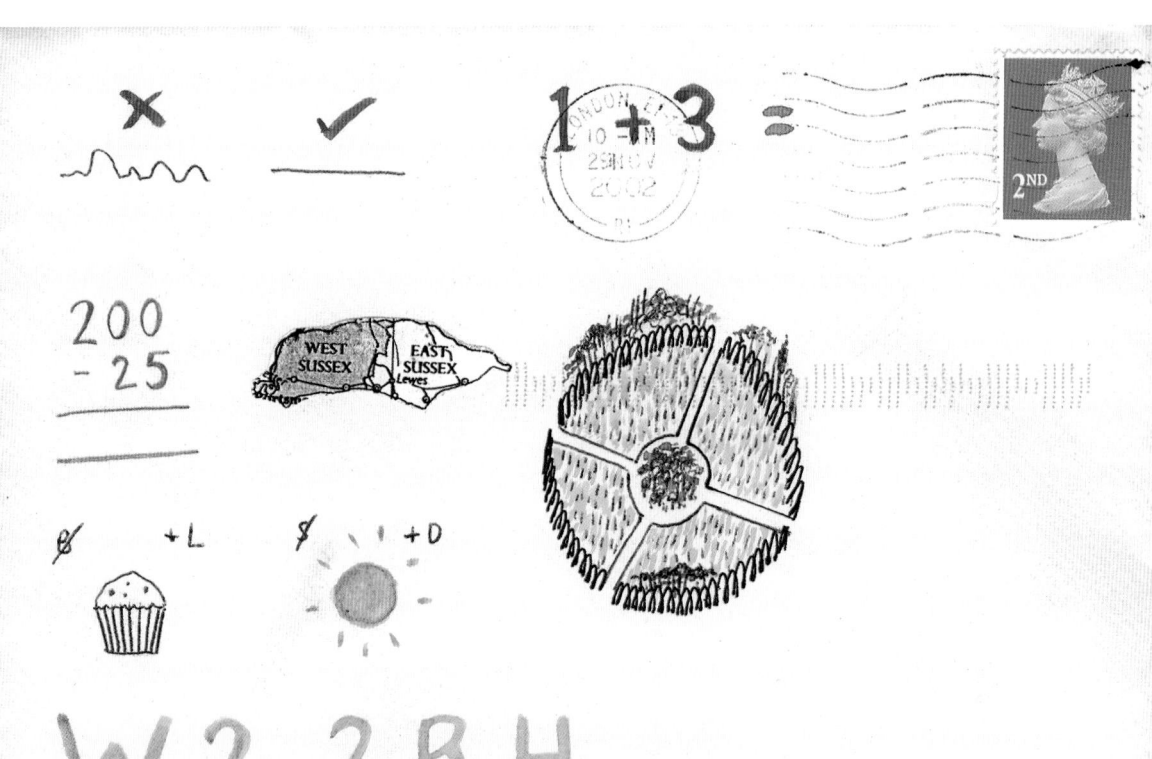

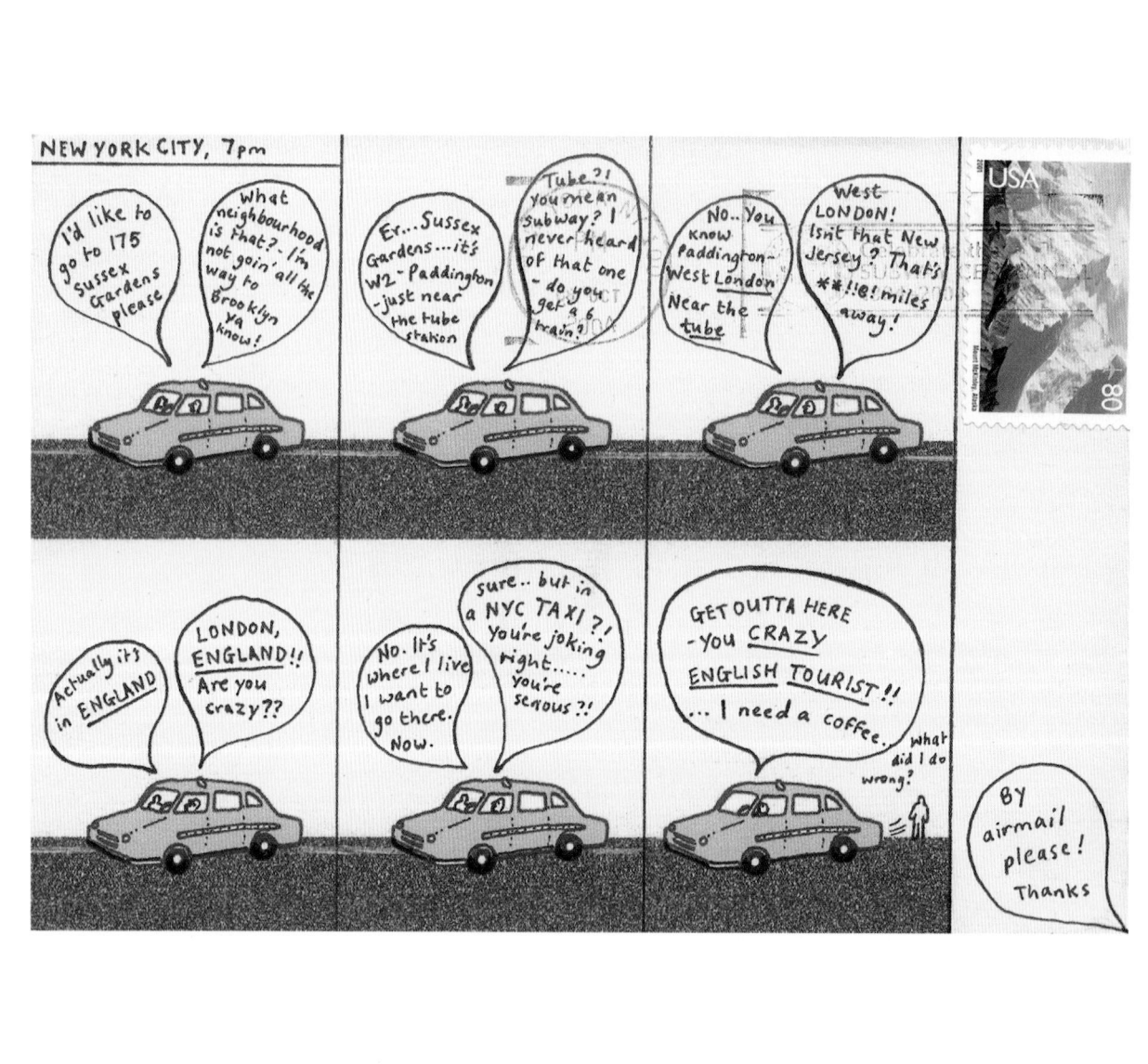

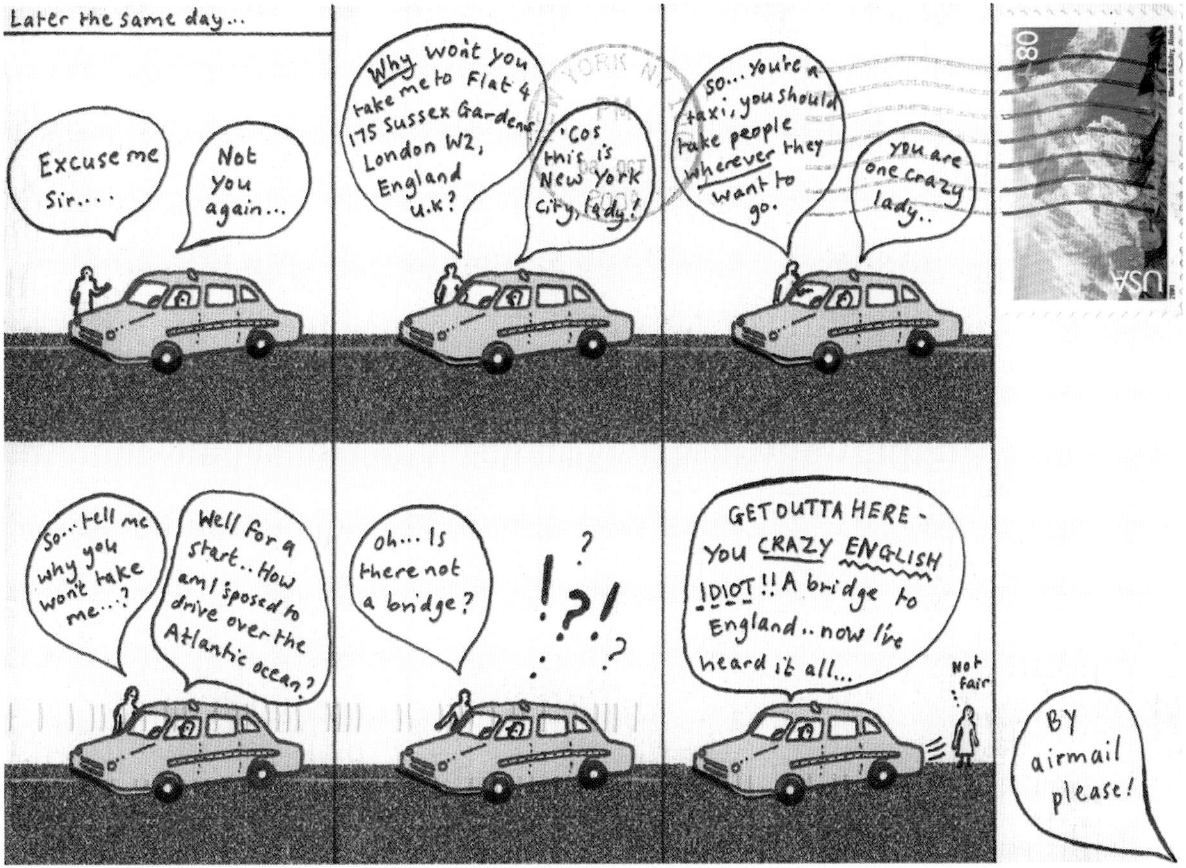
Later the same day...
Excuse me Sir....
Not you again...
Why won't you take me to Flat 4 175 Sussex Gardens London W2, England U.K?
'Cos this is New York city, lady!
So... You're a taxi, you should take people wherever they want to go.
You are one crazy lady..
So... tell me why you won't take me...?
Well for a start... How am I s'posed to drive over the Atlantic ocean?
Oh... Is there not a bridge?
!?!
GET OUTTA HERE - YOU CRAZY ENGLISH IDIOT!! A bridge to England.. now I've heard it all...
Not fair
BY airmail please!

Envelope fashion

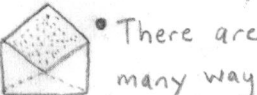

• There are many ways for the modern envelope to keep up with the current trends. Take a look at this exclusive range of patterns, available to wear on your inside↑

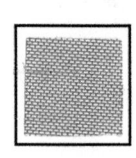 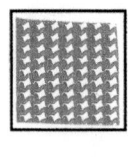 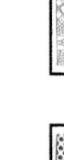 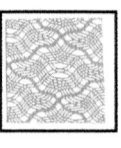

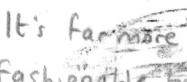
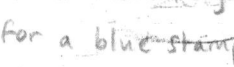

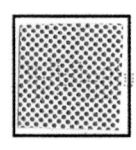

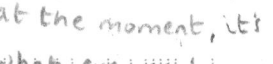

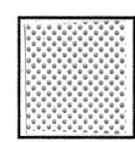

• It's far more fashionable to go for a blue stamp at the moment, it's what everyone's wearing!

• As for your address, London addresses are all the rage - we recommend the following : Flat 4 175 Sussex Gardens London W2 2RH

Hi there, I am an airmail envelope. It's quite a fun life - you get to travel a lot. On a plane. I really like to watch the inflight movies - and those food trays are really cool. I had chicken curry with rice yesterday - or was it today? - I get really confused with all this jetlag. Anyways, later I'm going on a _really_ long flight - all the way from New York to London! I am very excited. When I arrive I will ride the subway to Paddington and after that I'll arrive at Flat 4 175 Sussex Gardens London W2 2RH England. Awesome!

Gratin of Sussex Gardens with Flats and RH

Ingredients

4 Flats

175g gardens (preferably from Sussex)

1 large London

A pinch of W2

2 RH

Mix the 4 flats with a little water. Finely chop the gardens, making sure each piece is no larger than 1cm square. Fry them gently, adding the London after about 5 minutes. Add the mixture to the 4 flats, making sure to remove any lumps. Season with a pinch of W2. Finally, garnish with fresh RH, and serve immediately.

chemical structure of $f_2(lat)4$ (175) $\longrightarrow$ $Su_2(ss)_2$ ex_2 $ga_3(rd)en_s$

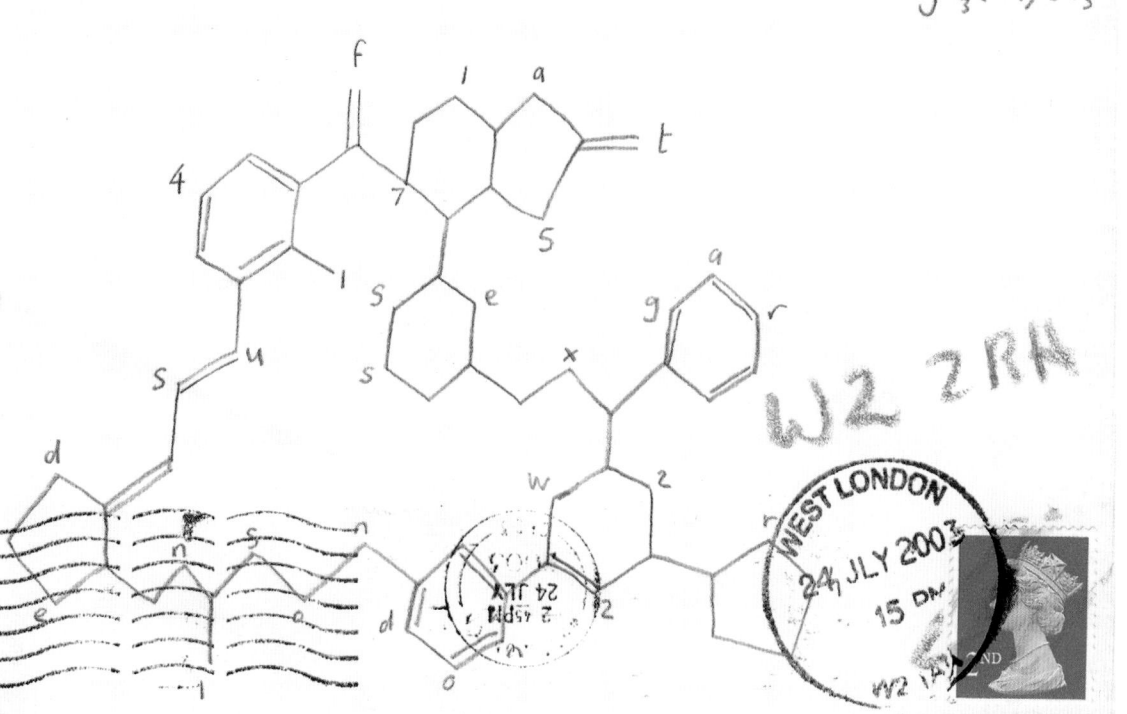

A black address in a coal cellar (look really closely!)

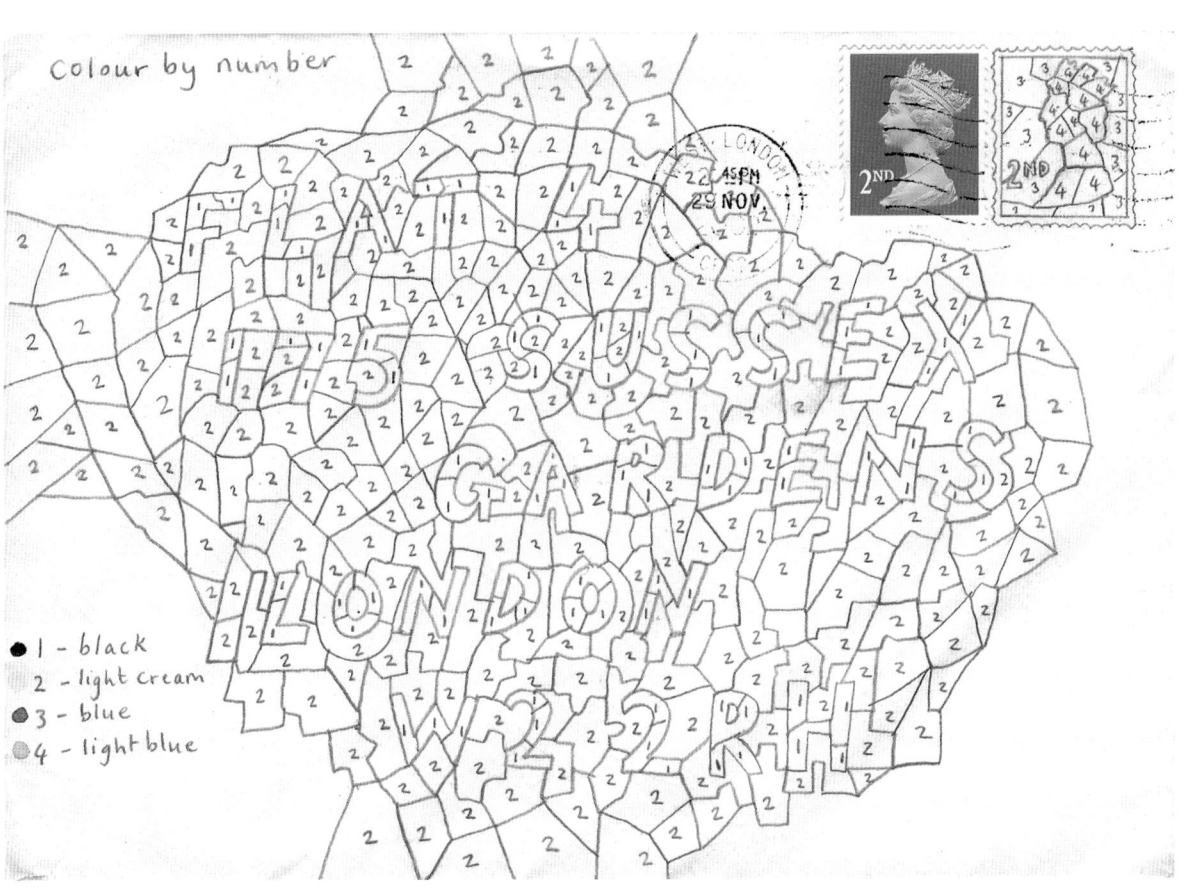

colour by number

● 1 - black
○ 2 - light cream
◐ 3 - blue
◑ 4 - light blue

173 Newark Street
wark Street 173 Newark Street 173 No
173 Newark Street 173 Newa
173 Newark Street 173
173 Newark Street 173 New
173 Newark Street
173 Newark St

A few others including:
1/1 173 Newark Street

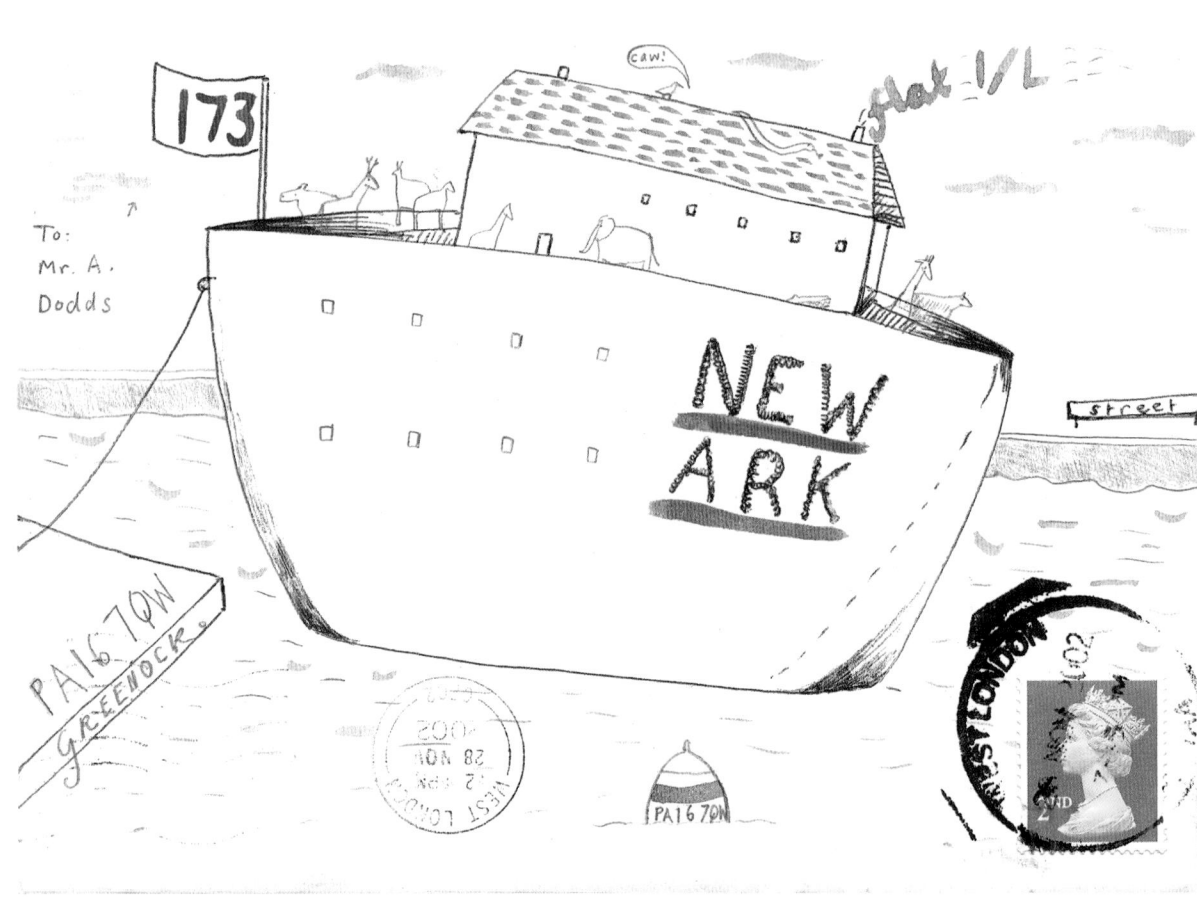

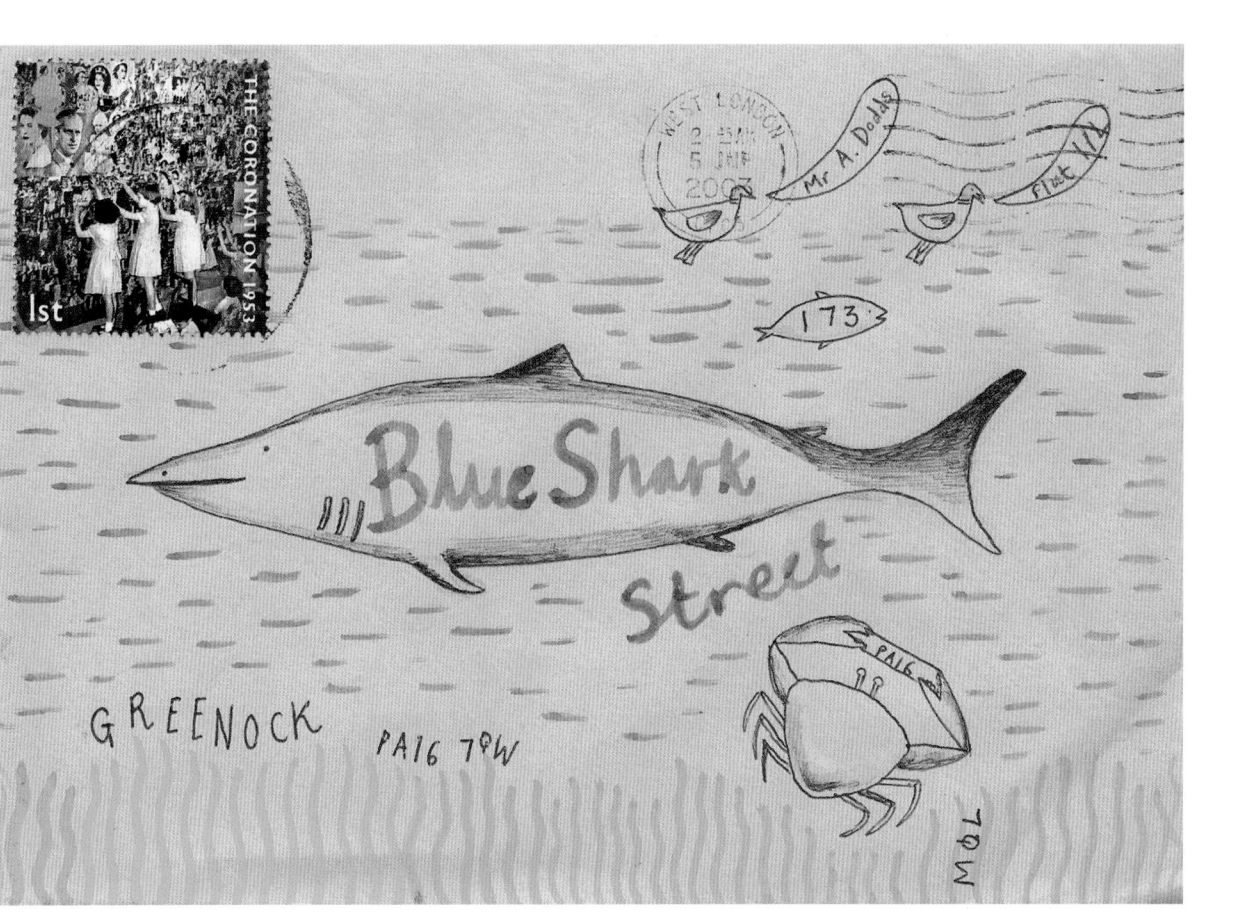

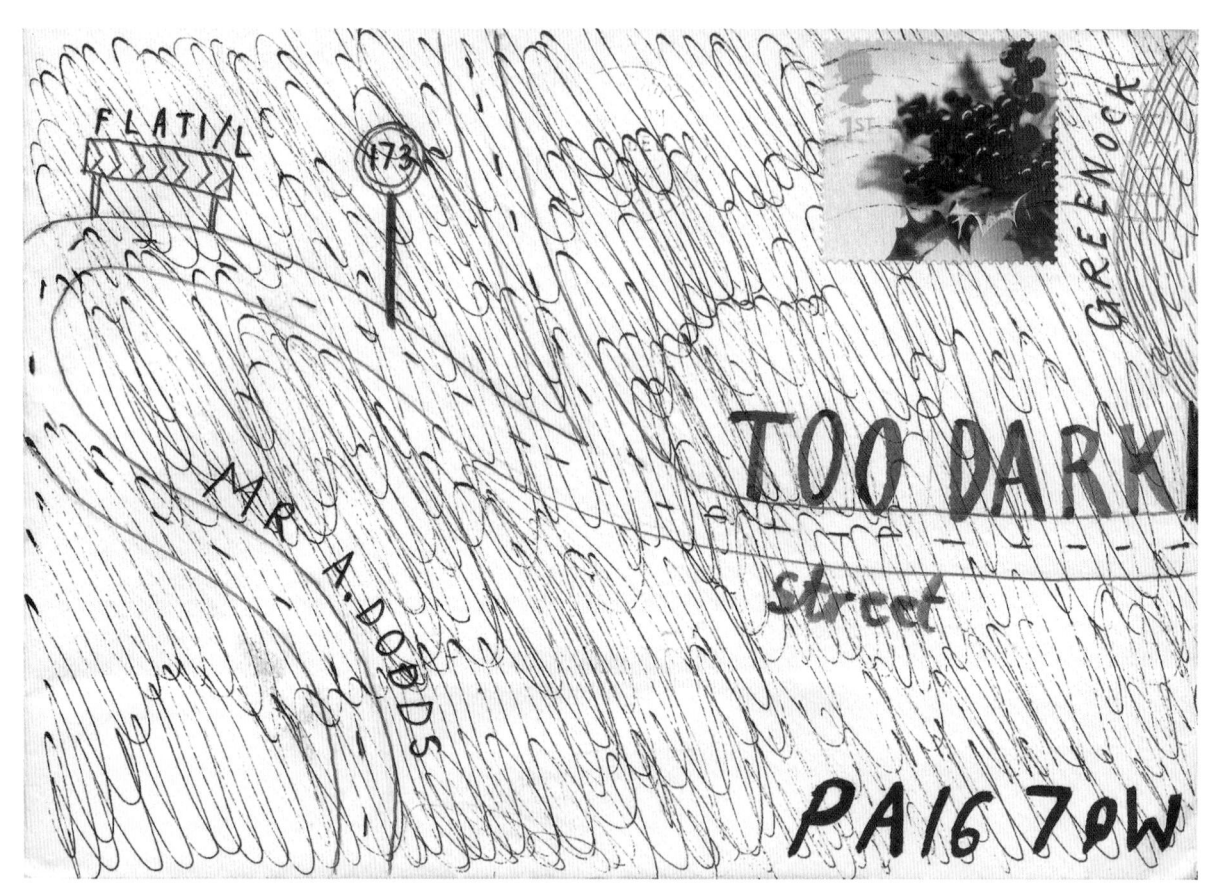

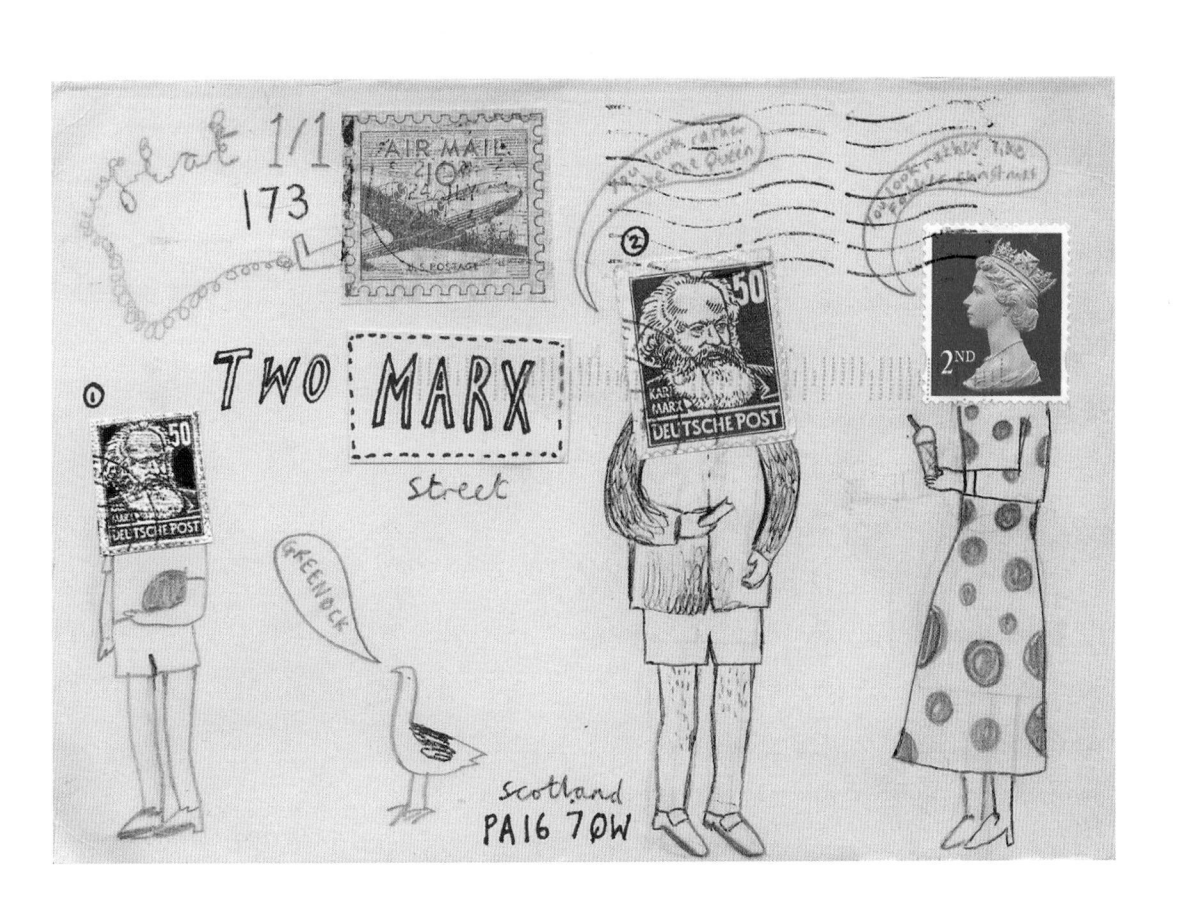

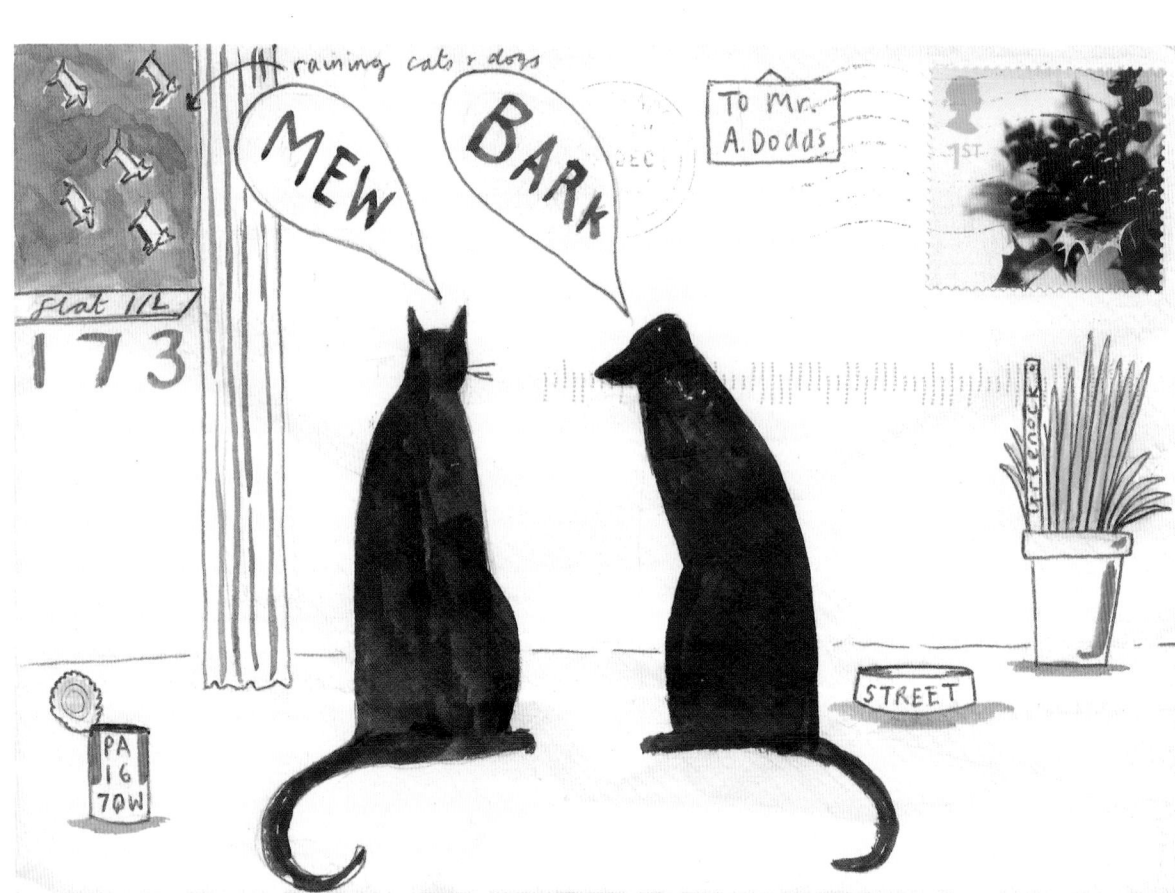

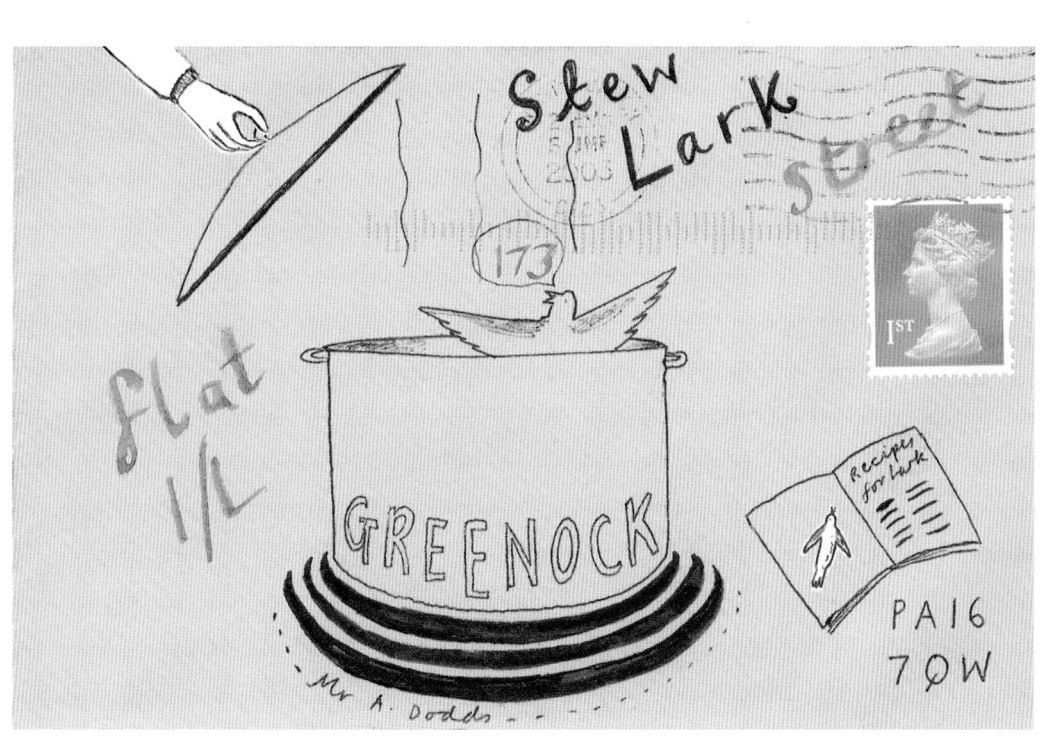

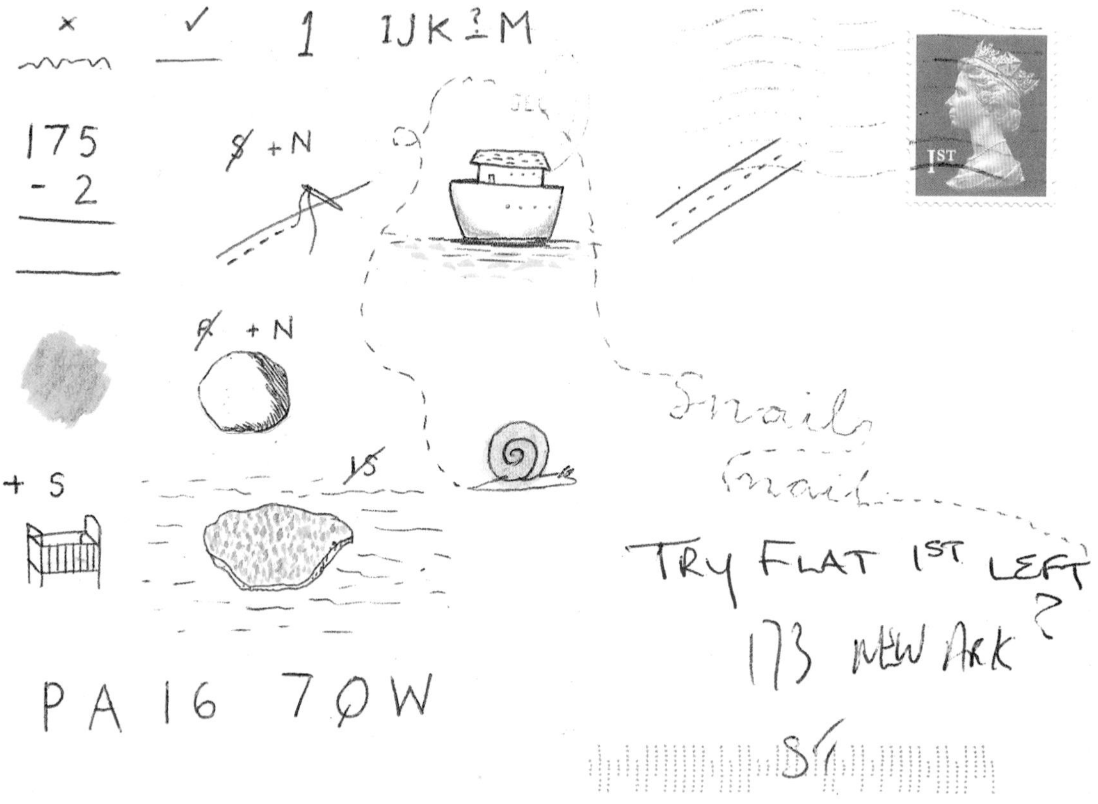

× ✓ 1 IJK?M

175
− 2

∅ +N

∅ +N

+ S

PA16 7ØW

Snail Snail

TRY FLAT 1ST LEFT
173 NEW ARK?
ST

26 = A

R.T.S.

21, 15, 26, 7   Z 15

Z T X   13, 22, 4, 26, 9, 16

8, 7, 9, 22, 22, 7

9, 22, 22, 13, 12, 24, 16   PP

26, A F   G 10 4

2ND

WE... ...N
24 JLY...
5 ...
W2 1AF

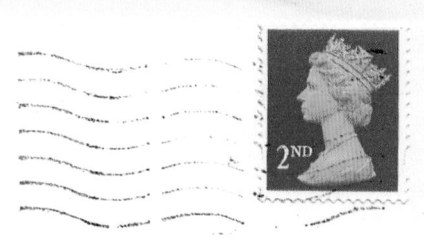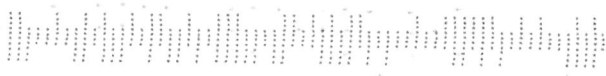

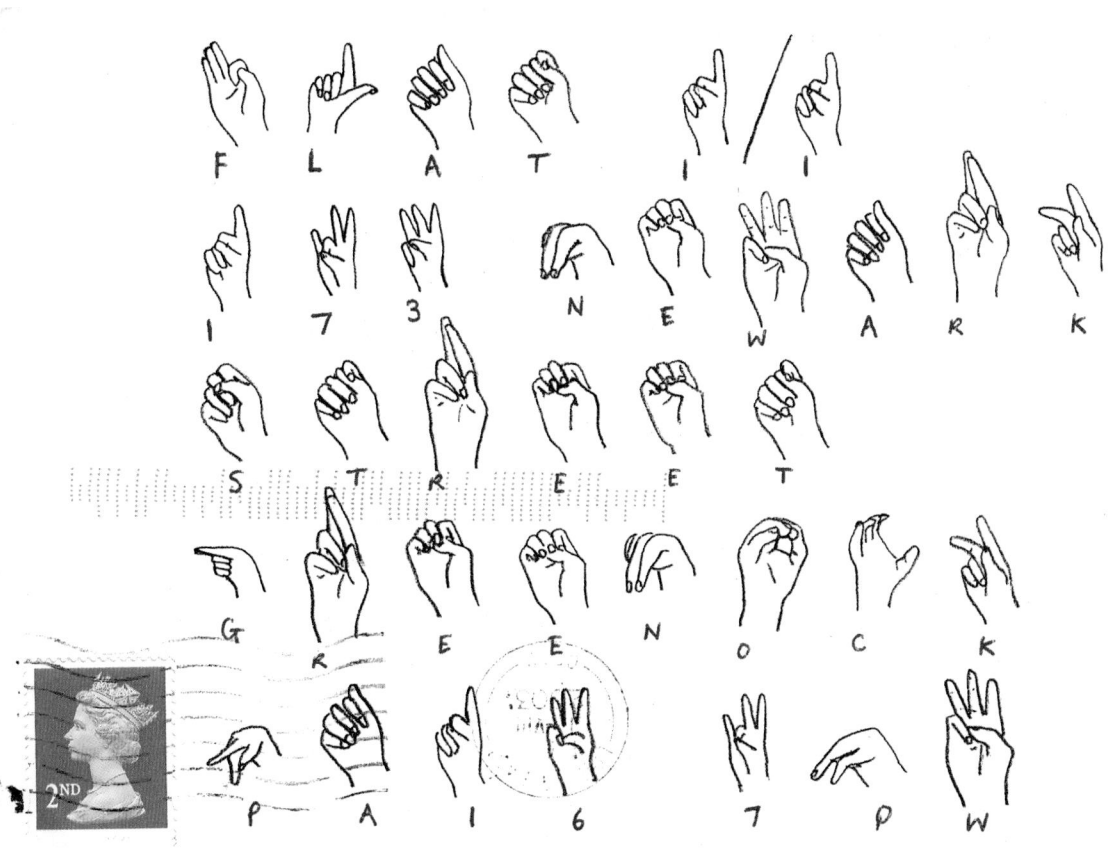

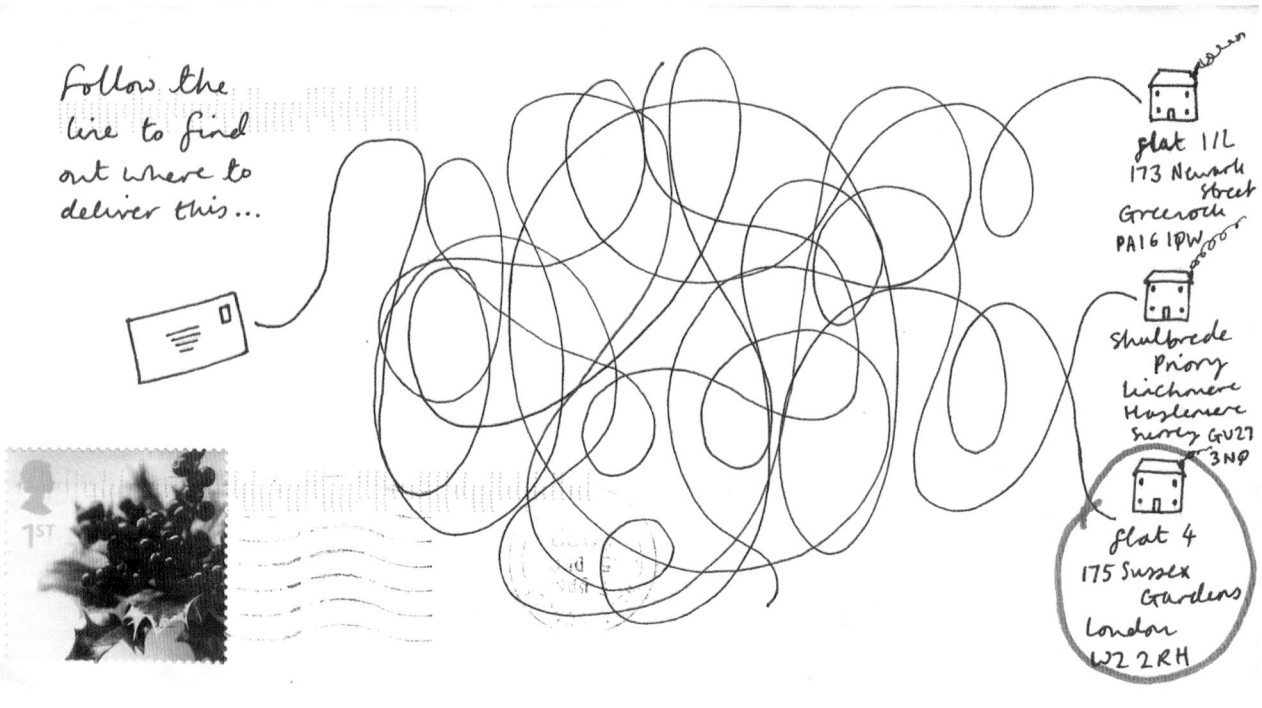

follow the line to find out where to deliver this...

flat 1/2
173 Newark Street
Greenock
PA16 1PW

Shulbrede Priory
Linchmere
Haslemere
Surrey GU27 3NP

flat 4
175 Sussex Gardens
London
W2 2RH

1ST

Sorry *To* say t*h*at this is th*e* LAST

*E*nvelope i*n* the book

How sa*d*!

ABOUT THE AUTHOR

HARRIET RUSSELL was born in London in 1977 and was brought up in a twelfth-century priory in West Sussex (with various cats, geese, and bantams). She studied visual communication at Glasgow School of Art and Central Saint Martins College, specializing in illustration in both courses.

She now works as a freelance illustrator in London, mainly within publishing and editorial. She is the author/illustrator of three children's books.

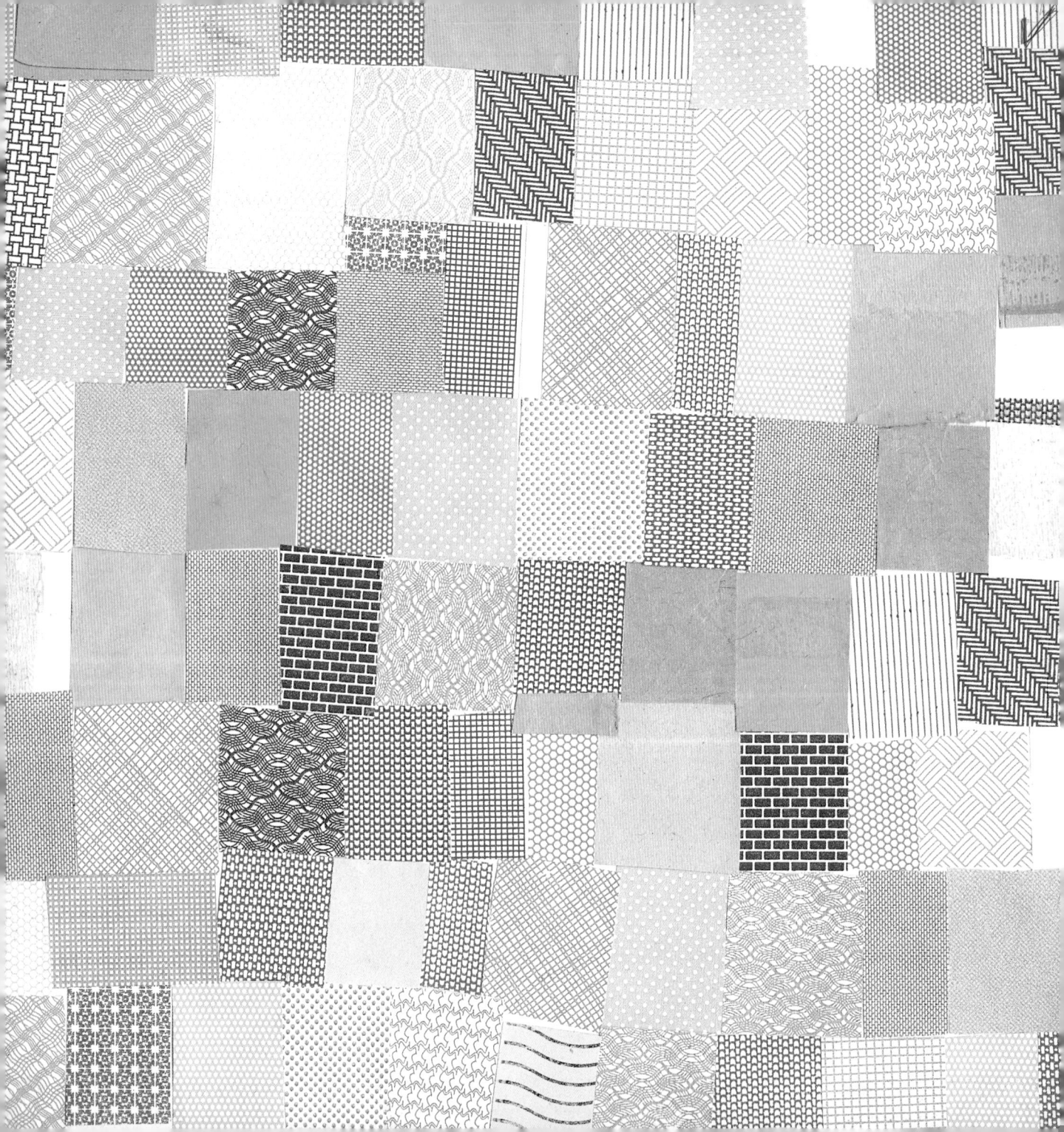